APPALACHIAN
HERITAGE

A SPECIAL DOUBLE ISSUE
VOL. 47, NO. 4
VOL. 48, NO. 1
FALL 2019 & WINTER 2020

EDITOR
Jason Kyle Howard

BOOK REVIEWS EDITOR
Emily Masters

STUDENT ASSISTANTS
Frankie Baldwin, Rachael Bates, Skylar Bensheimer
& Rhea Carter

MANUSCRIPT READERS
Katherine Scott Crawford & Patti Frye Meredith

ESTABLISHED IN 1973
PUBLISHED QUARTERLY
by Berea College
CPO 2166
205 N. Main Street
Berea, KY, 40404
www.appalachianheritage.net

The short stories in this publication are works of fiction. Names, characters, places, and incidents are either the products of the authors' imaginations or are used fictitiously. Any resemblance to actual events, locales, or persons, living or dead, is entirely coincidental. The views expressed in the creative nonfiction herein are solely those of the authors.

Electronic submissions only at www.appalachianheritage.net

Distributed by the University of North Carolina Press. Basic subscription price: $30/year for individuals, $40/year for institutions. For subscription requests and inquiries, visit the magazine's website, email uncpress_journals@unc.edu, or call 919.962.4201.

CONTENTS

INTERVIEW

CRAFT ESSAY

BOOK REVIEW

COVER PHOTOGRAPH

High Water by Greta McDonough

EDITOR'S NOTE

JASON HOWARD

W"hat is buried in the ground isn't always what you think. It's just the beginning." With these evocative, mysterious words, Annette Saunooke Clapsaddle begins to draw the reader into the world of Cowney, a nineteen-year-old Cherokee man who serves as the protagonist in her debut novel *Even As We Breathe.* He wants more than his hometown of Cherokee, North Carolina is able to offer, so at the height of World War II, Cowney moves to Asheville to work at the Grove Park Inn, where he finds himself caught up in a mystery and stigmatized because of his Native American identity.

While these words help to open Clapsaddle's tale of familial and cultural identity, they also serve as a metaphor for her deep, language-driven prose—and for the writing of her fellow featured authors. Alongside Clapsaddle in this special double issue, we are spotlighting Annie Frazier, author of the novel *Crazy House*, and Wesley Browne, author of *Hillbilly Hustle*, which will be published in March by West Virginia University Press.

In *Crazy House*, the reader follows Lizzie Robinson from her childhood spent in a doublewide in Raleigh, North Carolina, with a single mother, Burdette, to attending Duke University. After graduation, Lizzie opts to spend time in Connecticut with her boyfriend James as his wealthy, dysfunctional family unravels. There, she is moved to examine her own childhood and her relationship with Burdette. A graduate of Spalding University's Masters of Fine Arts in Creative & Professional Writing program, Frazier has written a novel that examines the complex bonds between mother, daughter, and place.

Browne's *Hillbilly Hustle* is something of a literary page-turner. Comic, noirish, and full of suspense, the novel tells the story of Knox Thompson, the owner of an eastern Kentucky pizza shop who spends his life hustling to tend to his business and parents. But things turn dark when he wins a backroom poker game. Knox descends into an underworld after being coerced into using his pizza shop as a front for dealing pot, putting his livelihood and family at risk.

In addition to our featured authors, this issue includes sterling, character-driven stories from Terrance Wedin and Jennifer Lee. Richard Hague returns to our pages with

"Scalpeen," an essay steeped in language and ancestral memory. Leatha Kendrick does double duty, contributing several poems and a craft essay on practicing mystery in poetry. We are also proud to include a series of bewitching poems from Tina Parker, an evocative poem centering on women in Chernobyl from Nicole Yurcaba, and numerous other poetic voices. For our interview, Clapsaddle joins bestselling novelist Silas House in a conversation from the 2019 Appalachian Symposium.

All of these contributions dig deep into the fallow ground of character and place. Read on: this is just the beginning. ∎

ANY CITY

TERRANCE WEDIN

Mom came downstairs, her eyes looking like she'd been crying all morning. I was still in bed, in the unfinished basement that was now my room. The leggings under my sweatpants itched. She barely ran the heat anymore. Getting out of bed meant getting ready for work—putting on the yellow Main Street Auto Spa t-shirt, the khaki shorts smudged with car grease. On the shirt, a turkey detailed a Corvette with a rag. It was always a conversation start if I forgot to take it off after my shift.

"They're taking the townhouse," Mom said. After spending our childhood in an apartment, my brother and I called it a house, even though it really was just a townhouse. After the divorce, Mom bought it on the cheap. Too good to be true.

Her work clothes were the same ones I'd always remembered her wearing, her haircut made her look like the Joan of Arc we watched in my experimental film class a couple years before. She'd worn her hair that way since my brother and I were born, said we never stopped grabbing it, so she just cut it off.

"Who's taking the house?" I asked, sitting up in bed.

"The bank."

"They can do that?"

"I've been behind," Mom said. "But I thought I could catch up."

She looked around the basement, my room since I'd moved back home. Cardboard boxes filled with books and clothes covered the floor. Two years and I still hadn't unpacked. I'd moved home after the car accident I'd gotten in right after graduating college—a windy back road, a broken jaw, a reconstructed orbital that swelled when the temperature dropped. When I was able to talk and move and eat again, the only steady work—besides the odd jobs I picked up for Riley—was at the new car wash. I hadn't planned on living there for long, just until I figured out my next move—maybe Philadelphia or New York, somewhere I could try acting or maybe make a film, I thought. But I'd never lived anywhere but my hometown. I didn't get on an airplane until I was almost twenty-three.

Then things changed. Dad had a heart attack. Then he got sober. It swerved all of us, him leaving Mom for a grad student and fleeing up the I-81 to Richmond. She'd tried leaving him a few times over the years, had us packed up in the backseat, duffle bags between me and Kent. But for some reason, she couldn't—even after some of the nights he'd come home and terrorize us, have us cowering in the back bedroom of the apartment like scared animals. After he left her, I didn't feel like I could leave, too.

"He had it out for me," Mom said.

"Who?"

"He knew this would happen, the economy."

She didn't name him anymore. During the divorce, she never mentioned the hurt he'd done to all of us over the years. She wanted the past to remain hidden, placid. *Irreconcilable differences* had been the official grounds submitted.

"You can't make the payments?" I said.

"I'm trying to catch up." She grabbed an unused extension cord off the floor and wrapped it into a neat coil.

"I can pay rent," I said. I had car wash money saved, a little more from the demo jobs I'd worked with Riley throughout the fall. I'd been attempting to save enough to move out, but then my truck would blow a tire or I'd spent it all at the bar and have to start over again.

"We should start thinking about the house as already gone," she said. "That's what the man at the bank told me."

■ ■ ■

At the car wash, they were cutting shifts. Some days I showed up in my yellow t-shirt and they'd let me clock in for an hour before sending me home. Washing your car was one of the first things that could go. The second thing, my manager said, was cosmetic surgery. "Cigarette sales remain strong," he said, smoking one outside the office. Almost every day people came to speak with him, resume in hand, only to get turned away. The jobs available in our area were jobs that didn't actually exist, that weren't jobs at all. Signs planted in the ground at traffic lights announced: *Work Available! Call Now!* Turn on the television or check online, and it was like the world was collapsing.

Recession.

Depression.

Foreclosure.

Bubble.

Occupy.

Crisis.

Unemployment.

One night, Mom and I ate boxed mac and cheese and watched a movie together. A tradition. The walls of the townhouse were bare. The living room was boxed, ready to be moved. Mom had found a cheap one-bedroom above the flower shop off Main Street. Now, she was just counting days.

Turn on the television or check online, and it was like the world was collapsing.

I was a little buzzed, but I didn't think Mom could tell. We were watching a black-and-white film, something foreign I'd found at the library. French boys in a schoolhouse gave the headmaster grief. I never drank in front of Mom. She didn't keep alcohol in the house, either. But during our movie nights, I kept a bottle of half-proof vodka in the back of the toilet tank—something I'd started doing after the accident. Dad had hidden his beers under the kitchen sink the times when he wasn't trying too hard to quit. I got off the couch and went to the bathroom to take a drink.

"I've been thinking I should move," I said when I got back.

"Move where?"

"Somewhere else, maybe up to DC or Philly."

"Oh," Mom said. "What would you do?"

"I don't know. Maybe do some auditions."

"Well you'd need a real job. You have to make money."

"I'd find something. Maybe marketing or something."

"I just can't support you," she said. "You know that."

"Kent will still be across town," I said. I couldn't remember the last time my brother had visited. Before his best friend jumped off a bridge, before yard signs and end time talks.

"I know you have to go. I know."

"There's just nothing here for me, Mom."

■ ■ ■

I checked on Kent across town. He barely left his apartment now that he'd lost his job at the dining hall. Downsizing, they said. He sat in his room eating ice cream and playing video games, and for money, I knew he had some scheme online involving gift cards. He'd stopped talking to anyone after Braxton left a note blaming his friends for his suicide. When I was still in school I'd stop in for lunch between classes and rehearsals sometimes to shoot the shit with the two of them, have them sneak me meals I couldn't afford.

At his apartment, his roommate let me in. Kent's room was ripe, pungent. Bottles of piss were lined up on his dresser. Finding a place to sit meant stepping over soiled clothes and dinner plates. In a year, he'd put on a hundred pounds and didn't look like the brother I'd grown up with anymore. I never knew what to say when I came to visit.

Kent sat at his computer, wheezing. He mashed keys with one hand, shifted his mouse with the other. On the screen, a tiny army moved across a wasteland and attacked another tiny army. Empty ice cream pints were stacked next to his monitor. Before my first surgery, Kent visited me once. He told me I looked like the Elephant Man, my face drooped and caved in. He started crying when I explained how they'd have to remove the broken bones in my face to fix it.

"Mom said she hasn't seen you in a while," I said.

"It's hard getting over there without a car."

"You know I can always come pick you up."

"Yeah, okay," Kent said. He hadn't looked at me once since I'd been in his room.

"You'd have to go check on her if I move," I said, picking an action figure off the floor. It was the main character of a space video game Kent and I had been obsessed with growing up. Both of us had been in shock when the hero took off the space helmet, revealing that she was actually a woman.

"The bank's taking the house," I said.

"What do you mean?"

"Mom can't make the payments," I said.

Kent stopped clicking at his game. The army on the computer screen stopped moving. "I barely get enough unemployment right now to survive."

"She didn't say anything about having to support her."

"I couldn't support her if I wanted."

"She's just worried about you," I said.

"I'm fine. I'm just living my life."

■ ■ ■

During college, I did a couple Beckett plays, and a Shepard one about brothers that people liked me in. The grad student who'd directed me had moved to Texas hoping to shoot commercials. She messaged me about the theater scene, the swimming, the Mexican food. She was done with theater. She had a job on a television show, getting actors coffee and wrangling extras. She said we all needed to move down there—that we could sleep on her couch. Six months later, she was headed to Los Angeles. After the car accident, I didn't do anything for a long time. I tried writing a play that took place in a small town, but I could never really get started.

I'd stayed around my hometown initially because I couldn't afford college anywhere else. There had been people from my high school who had left, but they always managed to end up back home. Eventually the idea of moving away to be some kind of actor or artist seemed fickle and false, a fantasy I'd be using to avoid real life. There was nothing I wanted in my hometown, only everything I felt a responsibility toward.

■ ■ ■

Mom had an interview for a second job lined up. Jockeying a register, second shift—something she could do after her day job as an administrative assistant at the college (one of the only reasons I got into school). The fast food restaurants where she'd dropped an application had accused her of being over-qualified. She knew someone at the drug store, someone who knew what kind of spot she was in.

Mom liked to tell this story about driving a forklift after college. She was making good money working the floor, waiting for Dad to graduate. Eventually he just dropped out, but still, she followed him. Her supervisor had tried to get her to stay on, give her a raise. She was the best forklift driver they'd had in years and the only one who kept passing the drug tests. She'd tell me it was the best job she'd ever worked, but she knew that it was time to leave, time to find something she could do with her degree. What she found was office work, a way of supporting her husband while he found his footing building sets for theaters.

Later that night when she got home, my empties were still on the kitchen counter. I'd passed out on the couch, woke when the chimes on the front door sounded. She considered the cans, crushed and halved. She dropped her office tote to the floor, then climbed the stairs to her room without a word. I moved the cans to the recycling bin, making sure I covered them with a newspaper. I mouthwashed, made sure my eyes weren't bloodshot. I'd only had a few, but I'd broken Mom's one rule—no alcohol in the house.

I knocked on her door, cracking it open a little. The reading light next to her bed was on. "What?" she said through tears.

"Can I come in?"

"What do you need?"

I'd remembered Dad standing in the same doorway, drunk, looking down at Mom on her knees protecting us...

"I just wanted to see how the interview went," I said.

I pushed the door open a little more, stood in the doorframe. I'd remembered Dad standing in the same doorway, drunk, looking down at Mom on her knees protecting us, my brother and I crying behind her. I wasn't sad about losing the house when I thought about that. I moved then, inside the room. The civil war history books that were usually stacked on her nightstand were boxed beside the bed. The pictures of my brother and I were missing from the nightstand. She sat cross-legged with a tissue in hand.

"How much have you been drinking?" she asked.

"Mom," I said, sighing. "I just had a couple. I'm fine."

"If you're drunk you should go stay at Riley's."

"I'm not drunk," I said. "I fell asleep."

"The girl interviewing me knew you from high school," she said. "I almost died. Can you believe that? She asked about you. Tonya. She said she was a cheerleader while you were on the football team. Do you remember her?"

"Yeah, I remember her, Mom."

"She said that I have a good chance at the job because I know Brian."

"So why are you upset?"

"Oh, because," she said, touching the tissue to her eyes. "Because I didn't think this would ever be my life. But here it is."

■ ■ ■

Riley called. He had good news and bad news. The bad news was that Dad had contacted him, wanted to know what his sons were doing. The good news was that Riley had some jobs he needed an extra body on—enough to keep us both busy for a long while.

I met him down at the bar where his daughter had been a waitress during college before she died. Drunk driver on I-81, coming back from a Dave Matthews concert at the Civic Center in Roanoke. A memorial plaque hung in her memory at the back of the bar, near the bathrooms, and every time we stopped in for lunch he made sure to polish it with a shirtsleeve on the way back from taking a piss. It hadn't surprised anyone much when he camped outside my hospital room for almost three days.

Riley picked at a basket of fries, a Diet Coke in front of him, the only guy at the bar without a beer. His Virginia Tech ball cap saved the seat beside him. In the beginning, before Dad bailed, Riley had been his sponsor. He was the only man I'd ever seen muscle Dad, a memory from my childhood, at some barbeque or birthday party. The image of my father pinned on the ground was still so vivid. When Riley was around I always felt safe.

I ordered a beer with my burger without Riley saying a word. He didn't care about being in a bar, or if I drank. Whenever I asked him how he knew about his problem, he always said he'd always known. Burying his only daughter was enough for him to call it quits.

"Talked to your mom the other night," Riley said.

"What'd she say?" I said.

"Said you were thinking about running away to be actor."

"Yeah, maybe."

"What if I told you I'd have enough work to keep you busy full-time? You still going?"

"Doing what?"

"Flipping foreclosures for the banks. A little paint, a little demo. Contract work, mostly. You know how many houses they're pulling every day right now?"

"Yeah, I know," I said.

"Hey, I'm sorry," Riley said, adjusting his ball cap. "I didn't mean to sound insensitive—she's better off out of that place, anyway. You quit scrubbing tires and stick around and I'll put you on full-time."

When Riley was still drinking, he and my Dad would come down to the same bar and scheme their way out of some money—Snap-on tools, industrial vacuum cleaners, football betting. The two of them split after Riley realized Dad was sleeping with his wife. In the end, it was Riley who had to let Mom know that Dad had left for Richmond, information he'd received from his ex-wife. After that, I think he felt some obligation to all of us, out of some shared guilt or shame or something.

"So where you going to hide out?" Riley asked.

"Thinking about Austin," I said.

Riley considered my answer, took a sip from his Diet Coke through a straw. "I'd understand if you left. Nothing much here."

I said, "I can't work for you for the rest of my life."

"What a fate that would be," Riley said, chuckling. "But who says you have to go now? With your mom and all. Maybe work a little with me, save some money. Maybe things will look different when you're working. Just think about it, yeah?"

Our bartender came over to check on us, asked Riley if he wanted another Diet Coke. He looked at her a little too long, then smiled. He said, "I'll spin off the planet if I have any more." The bartender rolled her shoulders back, faked a smile, looked for her barback. I wanted to tell her it wasn't what she thought, that Riley wasn't meaning to look at her the way he was. She could have been anyone working behind the bar and he'd have fallen into that trance, daydreaming his daughter back home, alive again. It was then that I knew how he saw me, finally.

■ ■ ■

A few days later, Mom and I packed the truck. We moved the first batch of boxes to a storage unit out near the industrial park. I chipped in fifty bucks to help with the first month's rent. The space was too small for all the boxes. Mom had kept our artwork from grade school, our old sports jerseys, yearbooks, old toys. What we didn't pack we put in a Goodwill pile or a trash pile. We sat with our knees on the concrete and picked through the boxes until we each had a box of things we wanted to keep, things we thought my brother might want, too.

I kept a picture I'd drawn of "The Big Hurt" Frank Thomas in third grade. My old McCoy's Auto baseball jersey. My

Nirvana *Nevermind* CD. My Legion of Doom wrestling figurines. A postcard Dad had sent Mom from the Epcot Center the year I was born. *The kid would love the palm trees. Stay warm. Love, Daniel.* The rest of my childhood was headed for the dump.

We moved the rest of mom's stuff into her new one-bedroom above the flower shop. During the day, the shop only listened to songs sung in French and you could hear the foreign words through the floorboards. With the second job at the drug store, mom wouldn't be home enough for it to really matter, she learned. A couple of days after she'd finished moving in they left a vase of daffodils on her steps, welcoming her.

After that, I tried messaging my old director about Austin. Never got a response. Keep Austin Weird. Bat City. Live Music Capital of the World. Longhorn Country. Violet Crown. Hippie Haven. I did some research, but really, it was just the idea of something different, something new. It was an idea. Looking back, it could have been any city.

I put my two weeks in at the car wash. They told me not to worry about the weeks, but asked if I could please return my t-shirt. I had a thousand dollars in the bank, and a truck filled with boxes and bags of clothes. I called Riley and told him he'd need to find somebody else for the job.

■ ■ ■

Dad called a couple days later. Riley had called and told him I was leaving. It was the first time I'd heard his cigarette-soaked voice since right after my accident.

"Riley told me you're drinking a lot," Dad said.

"Nothing I can't handle," I said.

"Okay, tough guy."

I thought about hanging up. The last time I'd seen him I'd been in a hospital bed. I'd waved him away. "Is that why you called?"

"Just called to say be safe on the roads."

"Will do."

"Okay then."

■ ■ ■

I tried not to think about my conversation with Dad when I told Mom I was leaving. Me and him, we weren't the same person. Not at all. I was different.

Then one morning, Mom and I walked out to my truck in the parking lot of the flower shop. She'd gotten me a bag full of snacks, cookies, drinks from the drug store. She hugged me and told me to call her when I stopped, to let her know I was still alive.

"And you know where you're staying?" Mom said.

"Yeah," I lied. "It's all set up."

"You can always come back."

"I know," I said, holding back tears. "It's a good thing, getting to see the world."

"We'll be here cheering for you."

"I love you, Mom," I said.

I waited for her to walk back up the stairs. At the door she waited for my car to leave the parking lot, waving goodbye as I drove off.

■ ■ ■

The plan was to drive until I got tired, stop somewhere, and then sleep. The directions I'd printed out at the library were folded in a journal mom had gotten me from the dollar store, along with some snacks for the road. But twenty-one hours to Austin meant I could make it in a day.

As I sped out of the mountains, leaving Virginia, I howled like a wolf with the window down. Nobody would know me in Texas. I could become anybody, anything. I could become the person I thought I wanted to become: actor, filmmaker, writer, artist.

I would become *somebody* down there.

I wouldn't come back. I wouldn't look back.

I hit Knoxville, Nashville, and then Memphis before dark. I pushed my little truck, testing its endurance. My old life—my Virginia life—fell away the farther I got across the country. After twelve hours on the road, I stopped at a rest stop outside of Fayetteville. Even at night, it was still in the high eighties out there. I made a bed in the cab of the truck with my comforter and pillows and blanket, took off my jeans. I kept the windows up because of the bugs, then cracked them because I couldn't breathe. I closed my eyes and tried to sleep.

Mosquitos swarmed. Tagged my legs, my arms. One of them even got into my underwear. The welts grew. I kept my eyes closed imitating sleep, but couldn't stop itching. A mosquito landed on my eyebrow and I smacked myself in the face hard enough that my ears rang after.

I didn't put my jeans back on. Just started the truck in my underwear and kept going. I turned the radio up, slapped myself a couple times. I had a little coffee left. Mostly, on the drive through the Bible Belt it'd been God and the market crash, but that night I got something good, one of those throwback stations playing songs I recognized, classic rock songs that were familiar, but still kind of strange. Songs that reminded me of Dad teaching me to drive.

The highway was dark and straight and hypnotic. The sky began going from dark purple to grey to light blue. I turned the music down. The film over the night melted away. I listened to the earth moving underneath me. I was out of coffee, but I didn't stop. I still had so far to go. I told myself I wasn't scared. But I didn't want to give myself the chance to stop and think about what was in that other direction. ■

POEM WITHOUT A GAZELLE

Waiting for the doctor for a room the latest
test results for the iv nurse to finally
thread the catheter into the vein
so the test can start for the valet to find
and bring your car for today's exam to say
you're doing alright at least for your age
Waiting isn't how I planned to spend
these years but then when did my plans
shape what happened except maybe as rowing
against the tide might help a person land
somewhere downstream oh well a gazelle
had been scheduled to show up a few
lines back to fill the drab and empty
waiting room door but Nannette appeared instead
in cheerful printed scrubs to say you were okay
the test went well and you know her voice and face
did give off something of the veldt's sere grace.

LEATHA KENDRICK

THE WARP

Everything rusts, warps, settles off-center
askew. I ask you, Is *this* what I meant
to make of myself? Except what's entered
the cracks in the smooth façade of my intent
is bright—unforeseen as moonlight's
body in the radiant dark. Rusted solid,
I am stuck in spots I had set all my might
against, unaware when love's slow heat oxid-
ized me to what I said I didn't want.
Bent to the daily *make* and *keep* of mother, wife,
I thought myself a "shrinky-dink"—the life
baked out of me, my juices spent. What went
was only blinding rush and noise. I'll take
what's here—loss and what it made of me, what it let me make.

LEATHA KENDRICK

AT THE GATE

Say you are not watching people take off
their shoes, put their belongings on
a conveyer, empty their pockets
of change. Say you are wearing

an extravagant silk scarf,
oversized sunglasses, a brilliant
smile. No searches stand
between you and the silver

jet warming its engines
at the gate. But
no. The men keep
taking off their jackets,

the line inches forward,
all of us barefoot, bare
headed, heading toward
more lines, the roll call

at each gate. There is no
elegant scarf, only a lavender
cardigan. No sunglasses,
just your private smile

at your daughter
planning her wedding and
your same blessed husband
hours ahead. No movie Idylwild
departure, but KCI's concrete

terminal—an actual
ordinary   life.
        [wonderful]

LEATHA KENDRICK

POEM FOR A DAUGHTER III

No snow today, no two below.
No diapers waiting in the pail for bleach.
No pail. No wooden house above the two-lane road,
no Freewill Baptist Church next door, no
cemetery on the point above our bedroom window.
No jewelweed, no damp dirt road rising in shade,
no poison ivy, no view of the Big Sandy as yet unseen
from the end of that trail. No weight, alive
in my arms, no new-broken ground thick with garden beans
wrapped in morning glory vines. Nothing twines here
except stillness broken by her call. They're not here
either, and yet
                    that baby and her daughter calling,
their tale about the broken washer fills the living room
with voices, brings back that forty-year gone snow,
the smelly pail, the garden beans, the jewelweed.
Changed bodies—hers and mine—marked by births
and deaths, bad hips, a grandmother's imperfect
spine singing down the chromosomes. What isn't
here? What is? This August heat, cicada whir,
a cricket by the door, and everything unseen.

LEATHA KENDRICK

SCALPEEN

RICHARD HAGUE

1

There is a racial memory by which the past is continually accumulated and preserved.

—*Henri Bergson,* A New Philosophy

Even before my father bought a remote parcel of brushy-up land in Appalachian Ohio's Monroe County (which land and the people living around it has become a major source of writing for me over a half-century) there was one place among many that particularly ignited my vivid youngster's imagination. Think of the enthusiasm of the boyish Mark Twain for a life on the Mississippi; I had something of the same enthusiasm, though more precisely a strange, sometimes overwhelming nostalgia, for some dimly-remembered but nevertheless emotionally powerful place and its concurrent life that, as a boy, I thought I could glimpse from my grandparents' front porch in Steubenville.

118 Logan Street stands three houses up from the river; about thirty giant steps could get me from the sidewalk there to the riverbank, and it was a journey I took often in my youth. But I remember equally as vividly sitting rapt in one of the metal lawn chairs on the gritty wooden porch my grandmother scrubbed almost every day, seeing maybe a half-mile away, as the crow flies, and three hundred feet atop the cliffs of West Virginia across from the paper mill, a lush green field sloping steeply downward, and from which I could not look away. In my imagination, I could feel the pitch of that far piece of land beneath me, feel the breezes that must have blown at that height. Oddly enough, I do not remember seeing Steubenville from that visionary point; and it is this detail which hints at the deeper remembering I suspect was going on during those long reveries.

James Cavanaugh Hague, my grandfather, and Helen Madigan, my grandmother, were descendants of Irish immigrants to Steubenville, their ancestors' earliest arrivals, as far as we can tell, slightly predating the mass exodus during the Great Hunger of the late 1840s. Despite there being only the thinnest shreds of information regarding our families in Ireland, one story survived. My Uncle Jack showed me a handwritten letter that said his great-grandmother, (this would be my great-great grandmother) Margaret Cavanaugh, sailed over as an infant in the late 1830s. She was fed fresh goat's milk during the voyage, and the ladle from which it was gathered and served had supposedly remained in the family long enough for him to have seen it as a boy.

I don't know: I never saw such a thing, nor did any of Jack's five kids, my Hague cousins, though I do have great-grandfather Richard's shoe last and cobbler's hammer. But the point is that the field high atop the West Virginia cliff, unfenced, steepening downward toward the edge, I did see, as if again, fifty years later. In May of 2015, my wife and I stood at the edge of the Cliffs of Moher on Ireland's southwest coast, dizzied not only with the beauty and height and sheer drop of them, but, for me, by an overwhelming sensation of déjà vu. Surely, somewhere in my DNA, or in the collective unconscious, whatever you want to call it, I was at a familiar place. That high, green West Virginia field of my boyhood was here; the Cliffs of Moher were back there, across the Atlantic Ocean and the Appalachian mountains and the Ohio River a half-century before, in Steubenville.

If this were the only such incident of such strong "racial memory," as a Jungian term names it, to strike me in my boyhood, I could write it off as just some sort of odd psychological phenomenon, the result of an over-active imagination working on nebulous speculations, perhaps even remnants of the fever-dreams during my boyhood bout with mononucleosis. But it isn't the only occurrence.

2

Life can only be understood backwards....
—*Søren Kierkegaard*

When I was about ten, my father built a concrete block shed, very solid, in our tiny backyard. A great pile of excavated soil lay next to where he'd dug the footers for the foundation.

After the concrete was poured and the trenches for the footers back-filled, the level grassless spot where the pile had been drew me to develop a project that lasted the rest of the season.

At first, I conceived of the excavation I began as a foxhole. However inaccurately or helter-skelterly, boys my age knew that our fathers had been at war not long ago, and the notion of foxhole, I suppose, enabled us to imagine fairly concretely a part of that experience. I dug with a short-handled shovel, as, I imagined, my father had dug in New Guinea, Okinawa, the Philippines. I piled the soil to one side like a berm. At last a crater-like hole, about a yard wide at its top and just as deep, flooded with sunlight in the sweaty afternoon.

But something was not right: this naked hole seemed unfinished; to slide down into it and just sit there created nothing in the imagination—no real sense of danger, no breathless battle fatigue, no thrill of combat, shells screaming

I dug with a short-handled shovel, as, I imagined, my father had dug in New Guinea, Okinawa, the Philippines.

overhead, no crazed enemy shouting banzai and hurtling atop me, his bayonet jabbing at my ribs, blood in his eyes, and haunting my nightmares for decades after, as it had been for my post-traumatic-stress-disordered father.

One day, I raided the pile of weathered boards dad had salvaged from a stricken barn out in the country and with which he planned to roof the shed. I dragged four or five to the hole and lay them over it; shoved tightly together, they looked like a trap door. I pushed a board aside at one end and slid through the gap into the claydamp darkness. Then, crouched inside, I shifted the board from below back into place, extinguishing the light.

This was more like it. I sat there, a tiny boy hidden in a board-covered hole in a backyard not far from an adandoned stripmine, not far from the hissing steel mills just over the hill, not far from the omnivorous river that vomited everything it carried into the sea—trees, broken dolls, wrecked boats— excepting only the swollen remains of the girlfriend I was to lose to it at the end of the next part of my life. In that backyard hole's dank enveloping, still a boy unacquainted with the darker chapters of life, I felt a strange, earthy safeness.

It was at least two decades later that I first learned about the scalpeen, a desperate temporary shelter built by displaced and starving rural Irish run out of their cottages and off the land by the English. The scalpeen, or scalp, was a shelter often constructed by laying sticks or branches over nothing more than a roadside ditch, some hole along the way. On that last day of the first part of my life I was re-enacting, though in full ignorance of it, the experience of my ancestors. In a kind of combined fore-knowledge and ancestral memory of the meanness, violence, and injustice of the world, I huddled, as perhaps some of my own realtives had, though in a womb-like darkness, calm, unformed and uninformed, not knowing I was soon to be delivered into the brilliant blast of light which is the knowledge of evil.

3

Through the study of history, we make the past usable,
turning handfuls of raw facts into meaningful narratives.
—Laura F. Edwards, Writing Between the Past and the
Present

This ending of what I might call the first part of my life had been held, undeveloped, almost entirely unexamined;

for all intents and purposes, unlived, if living teaches us anything, for six decades (though I have recalled it now and again during those nearly sixty years). Is it possible that many of our experiences, though vividly remembered, (or inherited from a distant ancestral realm, even from as far away and long ago as that archetypal galactic past of *Star Wars*)—is it possible that such experiences have yet to be smelted into what we might call self-knowledge, let alone wisdom? Is it necessary to write (or dance, or draw, or sing) about, say, such boyhood memories as I recount here, in order to discover (communicate, construct, compose, complete) their meaning?

Here, near the end of some part of my life, (I have just achieved the Biblical three score and ten), while at the same time headed inevitably— but not too quickly, I hope—toward another significant hole in the ground, I am pretty sure it is so. Art completes us; it is a way we have of recovering and understanding what seemed lost to time.

Our past is not past. In my case, at least, as long as there's more to be uncovered and gathered up, articulated—to be literally re-membered, from the dismembered bones of my family history scattered across windy fields both far off in Ireland and here in America—my past is clearly not finished.

4

Postscript

And so it is not. A couple of years after writing the above, I stumbled across, online of all places, the front-page obituary of my great-great-grandfather and in it the revelation of the existence of his first wife, my great-great-grandmother, both of whom I had until then known nothing about. I knew about Annie Butler, the somewhat infamous (though probably impatient of his drinking) wife of my great-grandfather and namesake Richard. It turns out the obituary was about his father-in-law, Theodore A. Butler, who died in June of 1907. He had come to Steubenville with his parents (they remain nameless and undiscovered to me still) from Hagerstown, Maryland in 1828. Most remarkable to me is this: "In early life he followed the river and has been over the river from Pittsburgh to New Orleans frequently." For a person who has all his life been a river rat, this came as a kind of genetic lightning bolt: if there is a rivering gene, I certainly have inherited it. Now I had an entirely new connection to the past, one that might lead to identifying at least one line of original Irish descent. Who were his parents? Who were his first wife Alice Moore's parents? Where did they come from? When? There is in all of this the same strange nostalgia, the longing for knowing these people and their lives, that I felt as a boy staring out over the river at that high green West Virginia field.

I do not know that other people have such an intense sensation of the past as I seem to do; I do not know what it means, exactly, either. Is it a response to my own life time so rapidly shortening? Or is it an intimation of the long time, the deep time, into which I myself will soon be plunged, to exist only in photos and words and memory, a few generations from now, perhaps, to drop into namelessness until the entire human family comes to an end? There is an exhilaration in considering such depths of time and such incredibly detailed but relentlessly transient remains of our days and lives.

We are involved in something really big here, and most of the time we miss it, either out of haste, or distraction, or denial. Only if we're lucky, as I have been, do we begin to experience intimations of it, hints that come to us as names, places, lost photographs, the little pieces of the family story, like that of Annie Butler's anger and of her throwing furniture out of a second-story window and setting it afire. It's that house, I imagine, that you can see in the upper left of the photograph above Theodore Butler's great-grandsons. James R. Hague is my father. This is the story as I know it now. How long this will be the "past," I do not know. Each new finding keeps it alive, growing back like an amputated finger in a magic story of renewal, the tale of a kind of family immortality.

Somewhere back there, an ancestor may have survived by digging a scalpeen. As surely as the river has entered my racial memory, so too has that grubby hole, out of which continues somehow to issue the family called Hague. ∎

SLOW HEAT

High strung
They called her
Unsettled
We come home
She'd clawed her a notch
Jerked the planks right out
Said the witch needed her.

Ginseng they said
Ease the hippo
Help her sleep
Start slow
Build the dose
None of us knew
What it would take
To smother her.

TINA PARKER

THE WITCH

We try the old ways

Wild geranium

To stop the bleeding

Devil's clothesline

For the burns and sores

But our apron strings fall

Loose our shoes will not stay

Tied the beds rise up

We wind up on the floor

The clothes hung on the line

Torn off till all we can do

Is spread ourselves out on the grass

And wait.

TINA PARKER

CONVERSION

I saw I had to go down to the devil's hell
That was my home. I didn't want to give up
Worldly things but when the Lord got me ready
I came leaping and jumping. I fell down on my knees
And said "Lord if you will save me
I'll do anything you want me to do."

Of course he sent me to the yellow split level
At the edge of a farm
When I was a child I spoke to the horse
At the fence, fed it sugar cubes
When I was a child I thought I was saved
I read Revelation. The horse was a white horse
Clothed in a robe dipped in blood
His name was The Word of God
And I was the rider named Faithful and True.

High-headed people, I tell you
Sometimes it's hard to get humble
I'm no longer a child
I don't care for the things I used to love
The farm is row after row of houses
The horse is a pale green horse
Out to kill with a sword, with famine
And pestilence. There was never anyone
Who could save us.

TINA PARKER

TESTIMONY

They told the judge
I sat before an open fire
Fell right into it
But wasn't a hair on my head singed.

They recalled my vision
A prophetess wearing clothes
The color of rotten grasses
Grounding sage to a fine powder
They said I put it in their tea
Told them to drink
And be sanctified
Said their throats burned
Claimed they could not speak.

The minister said he'd seen many
Slain in the spirit but not me
Said I was different
That he felt directed to sign
As witness.

TINA PARKER

REDEMPTION

The minister says I'm alive

Through grace says

They may never know

What rendered me silent

He tells them to pray

The spirit gives several messages

In other tongues

> *Praise the Lord*

> They shout

> *Praise the Lord*

The women place a Bible

Under my pillow I dream

My voice returns

I point to the minister

But no one listens.

TINA PARKER

COVER THE MIRRORS,

I told them

On and on they hollered

In prayer

Their palms pressed

 Oil to my forehead

    I'll fly away oh glory

    I'll fly away in the morning. . .

They faked my healing

I cannot account for what evil

May enter.

TINA PARKER

AN *APPALACHIAN HERITAGE*
INTERVIEW

ANNETTE SAUNOOKE CLAPSADDLE

When it is published later this year, Annette Saunooke Clapsaddle's debut novel will mark a milestone in American and Appalachian literature. *Even As We Breathe,* which tells the story of a young Cherokee man struggling with the limitations of his community and the prejudice of the outside world, will be the first novel authored by an enrolled member of the Eastern Band of Cherokee Indians and published by a major press.

The story had been bubbling inside Clapsaddle for some time after her first manuscript was a finalist for the prestigious PEN/Bellwether Prize but ultimately went unpublished. Onstage at Berea College's third biennial Appalachian Symposium in mid-September, she recounted her shock when she received the offer of publication from Fireside Industries, the new literary imprint and joint venture of the University Press of Kentucky and Hindman Settlement School. It took a while for the news to settle in with Clapsaddle, who teaches English and Cherokee Studies at Swain County High School in North Carolina. But when it did, she celebrated with Mexican food and champagne, then immediately set to work on revising the manuscript with her editor, Silas House.

When it came time to give her reading, Clapsaddle's lyrical, image-driven prose, delivered in a steady voice, held the audience of students, professors, community members, and fellow writers captive—no small feat when considering she was featured alongside bestselling novelist Charles Frazier and acclaimed Americana singer-songwriter Dori Freeman. Later, Clapsaddle participated in a public conversation with House that examined the intersections of Cherokee and Appalachian identity, erasure, native and rural bias, and media representation. The conversation has been edited for length and clarity.

■ ■ ■

SILAS HOUSE: Great writing, especially [in] novels, must begin with a balance of mystery and emotion. [The opening to *Even As We Breathe*] is just packed with emotion, packed with mystery, and it makes you want to keep reading the book. What is the book about?

Annette Saunooke Clapsaddle

ANNETTE SAUNOOKE CLAPSADDLE: *Even As We Breathe* is half set at the Grove Park Inn in Asheville and half in Cherokee, North Carolina. During World War II, the Grove Park Inn held access diplomats and foreign nationals as prisoners of war for just a couple of months one summer. And so that's the backdrop for the story when the main character, Cowney, a Cherokee nineteen-year-old boy or man—depending on if you ask him or someone else—goes to work [in maintenance] at the Grove Park Inn. And along with him, a young Cherokee woman named Essie travels with him to go work at the inn as well. While he is there, he's accused of being involved in the disappearance of a diplomat's young daughter and so, while he's trying to exonerate himself, he's also working through issues of his own personal identity back home [in Cherokee] within his own family structure and [he] finds his way.

SH: Erasure is a big theme in the book. [When I teach Appalachian literature], we always focus on displacement, [which is] a kind of erasure, of course, and we start with the Cherokee and we look, in particular, at the Cherokee Removal. That informs the whole rest of the class and we keep coming back to the Removal and all those other displacements that have happened in the region. When you live in a place where an attempted genocide has occurred, like the Qualla Boundary [in North Carolina]... it gets in your blood and bones even if you don't know it— even if it's in your subconscious.

ASC: I absolutely agree with that, and I think it is important to connect our Cherokee experience with our Appalachian experience. Specifically in Swain County where I teach, we have the famous "Road to Nowhere," which is a road that was never completed after a community, Fontana, was flooded by the TVA. There was an agreement that the federal government would finish the road so folks could visit road sites. So we have a long history of broken promises, unfortunately, in our area and I think that, in some way, connects us to even non-Cherokee folks that live in far western North Carolina.

With that history of genocide comes a sense of distrust with the federal government and it influences everything we do, and it also influences, specifically for Cherokee, how we protect who we are and our identity and what we've worked to regain from that attempted genocide. I think some people get frustrated when they come to visit and we don't welcome everyone with open arms and we hold back some critical cultural knowledge and things like that, but it is out of sense of protection for that long history of knowing it can be lost really easily and also taken advantage of. That's kind of the darker side of that history.

It has also kind of separated us from our brothers and sisters, almost literally. There are three federally recognized Cherokee tribes. There's us, the Eastern Band; there's the Cherokee Nation in Oklahoma; and the United Keetoowah band in Oklahoma. We are historically one tribe, but we function completely separate now and that's a result of the Trail of Tears. However, I think that is also a testament to our strength and resilience; we can weather just about everything. When you beat off genocide, you can have a new perspective on the trials of life, politics, and history. We have, as a community, known the importance of holding on to our cultural values. Everything else will change, but we can maintain [who we are] if we hold onto our values.

That's become an important lesson for us, moving forward. And then also I would say…a sense of humor comes out of communities that continue to fight for their existence and try to find peace in life, what we call *tohi*, which is just a sense of peace with your existence. Sense of humor is such a big part of that.

SH: The whole time you're talking, I'm thinking about how that is so similar to being Appalachian, right? That constant, attempted erasing. The Cherokee [were the first Appalachians and], to a large part, had their language taken from them. People weren't allowed to speak the language, and we still see that happening today for Appalachians. I have students all the time who tell me that they were made to lose their accent so they could get a job, or [so] they could get in a certain class or a certain club at school. I love [considering] the Cherokee experience, especially because…that just keeps happening. It's all these hundreds of years later and people are still attempting erasure. On one hand, we have this whole thing where everyone wants to be Native American, right? But at the same time, there's still that erasure that happens. In what ways do you see that happening today?

ASC: There's a systematic erasure. In terms of our sovereign identity, most people don't understand that or where that comes from, and that can be confusing for people. On the other hand, there is this individual need to find community. Specifically, for Americans wanting to find their farthest link back to this land and a narrative that is very common, especially in Appalachia, the historical lands of the Cherokee, is that people have Cherokee ancestors. I understand the need to try to find that community through that. It's a constant balance between—I hate to say people, that's so general, [but] society not understanding why we operate as a sovereign government. At the same time, individuals want to identify as Cherokee, but not the complexities of [being] Cherokee. They just want that ancestry and maybe don't understand all of the government responsibilities and all of the values of the community. So it is definitely—we're a community that's misunderstood. I don't fault [that]—everyone should want to be Cherokee. I get it, we're so cool! But there's a lot more to it for us than researching history.

SH: One thing *Even As We Breathe* does so beautifully is show Cherokee characters [as] human beings who happen to be Cherokee, instead of the other way around, right? What are the biggest misconceptions you encounter about Cherokees or native peoples?

ASC: Part of this, I always have to admit, is a little bit our fault because we had to make a living. So with our tourism industry there are stereotypes that have been perpetuated, and luckily in the last decade or so, we're [doing] a really good job of trying to remove that from our public identity. The basics are around images in terms of colorful headdresses, and [that we] lived in teepees. None of that is true. We lived like probably your ancestors lived in Appalachia, in log cabins and [we made] use of the land. So any time you see [that] imagery, it doesn't quite make sense, right? It doesn't make sense for you to live in a teepee in Kentucky. It doesn't. I don't think there [were] buffalo herds. There are elk...

We were a permanent settlement. So the imagery things are definitely a misconception. But I think—and this is true for natives and native literature—this idea that Indian people are somewhat magical. There are no magical qualities to being a native person. There are misconceptions that we are more in tune with nature and those are kind of like the good qualities, right? Those things that seem positive on the surface, but they can be very detrimental. And then there are also the negative stereotypes that come along. I like to think about literature a lot; [there is] the early literature stereotypes of very violent Indian men oversexualizing Indian women and then the more modern stereotype of the drunken Indian. We see—I think in Appalachia in general we see substance abuse becoming more and more of a stereotype of our people, and that's something native communities deal with as well.

SH: You were educated at Yale and William & Mary, so I'm wondering if you could talk a little bit about how you were received there as a rural person and as a native person.

ASC: One of my favorite stories to tell about Yale and one of my early experiences as a rural, southerner—I guess that's part of it too—[is when] I was in a sectioned class. So, you have lecture and then you go to section with your [teaching assistant] in this small group setting. I was an American Studies major [and] we were having a discussion about folks like the Vanderbilts and Carnegie and all those guys. I don't even remember what the question was, but I made a comment about one of them being rich and a young man, not from where I'm from, looked at me and said, "You do realize the difference between being rich and being wealthy, don't you?" My freshman self, I looked at him and I said, "Nope. Because where I am from we are neither."

The discussion went on and I remember leaving—I was still embarrassed when I left—and I was walking back to my dorm.

I was the manager for the women's basketball team and one of the guys from the men's basketball team caught up with me and he goes, "Don't worry about that guy. He's just trying to sound smart."

Yale is a wonderful, welcoming space, but you've got people from all over and the first thing...they hear is an accent and then they also have absolutely no idea who a real native person is. I was a part of the Native American Association at Yale and every year we put on a pow-wow, which is a contemporary celebration. This is not a traditional thing, but [a] festival that lots of cultures have and we [had] gone to meet with the dean at the time... about some particulars and funding and all that good stuff that student groups deal with, and my best friend in college [was] from Rosebud, South Dakota. And we're walking into the dean's office with these huge doors—just like you'd expect the dean's office at Yale to look like, right? These huge doors open and we walk in and above the fireplace is this gigantic portrait of Andrew Jackson. So I looked at my friend and I said, "This is not gonna go well."

So you know, [there was] a lot of being in places where I was expecting to get an education, [but where] I did a lot of [the] educating, and so did my other peers from other tribes. William and Mary—within a year or two of getting my Masters there I served in kind of an advisory role because they changed some of their imagery of tribe and we had some conversations about that process too.

To really understand people, it takes time and conversations, and when people are willing to do that then I found communities of acceptance. And people who aren't willing to do that—I'm not sure I want to be part of their community anyway. It just takes open dialogue and, as I keep coming back to it, a sense of humor because people have not had the same experience I've had. I grew up in the tribal community and that's really, really rare in this country. I keep trying to remind myself of that often too.

SH: What are some of the worst representations in the media that you notice?

ASC: I know this is always controversial but I'll say sports mascots, number one, because they're such caricatures of native people and because of the mentality of competition often times uses others for its teams' mascots in violent ways. They hang mascots and you see someone who's supposed to represent your people being hanged. That's horrific and I can't believe that still goes on. Names like "Redskins"—there's no way for you to explain that one away to me. That's something that's still okay in 2019.

I'll say, probably the other one is the sexualization of native women through especially Halloween costumes. [Autumn] is really difficult because of Thanksgiving and Halloween and the images that get portrayed through both of those holidays. I'm sure most of you are aware of the real media push to acknowledge missing and endangered native women in this country. When I see a Halloween costume that like an oversexualized Pocahontas, short leather skirt, that—to me there's no excuse for that.

SH: Is there good representation out there?

ASC: Yeah, I think there is. Again, I think when media or Hollywood or society understands native cultures, then they understand the sense of humor. There are examples of shows that will have native characters and what I always look for is if that character has that sense of humor. Not everyone agrees with me on this one, so people will disagree—when Johnny Depp played Tonto in *The Lone Ranger* a lot of people didn't like it. But I loved it because that was more real than anything. His sense of humor and the wit and the different world view on how to tackle a problem. There are problems with that movie; there are problems with Johnny Depp. [But] I think it's a good representation of native culture when it's a human representation of native culture—that it's layered [and] unexpected in some way just like any other character. ■

AN EXCERPT FROM

EVEN AS WE BREATHE

ANNETTE SAUNOOKE CLAPSADDLE

About the place—when I take you there or when you find it on your own, just know that what the old folks say is true. This land is ours because of what is buried in the ground, not what words appear on a paper. But also know this: what is buried in the ground isn't always what you think. It's just the beginning. It's the beginning of the story— the beginning of all of us who call ourselves

Homo sapiens. Fitting, I guess, that what I found buried, just as I was trying to figure out how to become a man and still be human, was the very thing that threatened to take it all away. Just when I began to see what taking control of my own life might look like, I realized I was not who I thought. And neither was this place.

That summer in 1942 when I met her, really met her—before I found myself in a white man's cage and entangled in the barbwire that destroyed my father, I left the cage of my home in Cherokee, North Carolina. I left these mountains that both hold and suffocate, and went to work at the pinnacle of luxury and privilege—Asheville's Grove Park Inn and Resort. I guess I had convinced myself that I could become fortunate by proximity—escape Uncle Bud's tirades and my grandmother Lishie's empty kitchen cabinets just by driving a couple of hours up the road. It sounded good to tell folks I was raising money for college; but the truth was, I didn't know what I was doing. I just didn't want to do it *there* anymore. And if I stayed any longer, I would become rooted so deeply I might as well have been buried.

My plan didn't quite work the way I thought it would. When I got to the resort, I mostly stayed outside, cut the trees, mowed the grass, and helped to dig the holes that would sink signs and posts for barbed wire fences. Music occasionally seeped from the Ballroom, but was muted by thick, lead-paned windows before one note ever reached the perimeter of the property.

That's where I first found the bone. I was on my hands and knees, pitching rocks and digging holes. It was just as the inn, like its music, was becoming dulled by wartime restrictions and hushed by lead bullets. The prisoners—who were actually diplomats and foreign nationals treated more like guests—weren't really known to me yet. That little girl, God bless her soul, had barely even stepped foot on the property and I was still as free as I would ever be.

I squatted there by the fence along the boundary of the Grove Park property and grasped the bone by its middle, pointing both ends upward, studying its curvature. A bent bauble for my idle adolescent hands to fidget with in absence of a ball stick or soldier's rifle. I can't recall playing with many toys as a child. That's probably why it spoke poetry to me as a young man.

The bone was smooth and porous, its slight c-curve angled in motion, calling to be grasped, used—a weapon, at least in some primitive function of strength—like a sub-human scythe, though innately human. Maybe even the very core of humanity. And, now, as I recall the moment out loud, it was an embarrassing indulgence of make-believe for a nineteen-year-old. It's all right to laugh. I don't blame you.

Such an extraordinary object to be inside any amount of flesh, it was wholly earthen. Not sterile or cellular. It was natural in a way we pray our body is not.

Momentary. Seasonal. Destined for expiration.

The bone had lost its story. Petrified into a mere alkaline deposit, transient and nameless.

I was immediately spellbound by this calcified opportunity to embrace a remnant of a life's existence in one hand. Dry it. Dust it. Preserve it, and listen. Buried by a story and I was the only one on this earth privileged to hear it. "Cowney," it seemed to coo my name like the beautiful girls of my daydreams, the ones who never took interest in boys like me. Just as I was yet to know of a certain beautiful girl's power, I was yet to understand the power that bone would yield over my life. I was yet to know how much more I would risk for her, for it.

I am bits and pieces of the people I meet, my teacher once told me, though more accurately, of the people and places and creatures. And so, because of that summer, and that war and that small, hollow relic, I am bits and pieces of a grand estate, and a half-tamed primate, and a dozen accents, and a missing girl, and a fearful girl, and all the trees and mountains and asphalt in-between.

And you—well, I reckon you will be, too soon enough.

■ ■ ■

Knowing that she is now gone from this earth, all I am left to do is wonder what remains of her here... for me... for anyone who knew or didn't know her. What happens to the memories? How long do they survive? I can still see her, dancing. Head thrown back laughing. If there's one thing old age has taught me it's that there are many kinds of love. She taught me that sometimes we feel many different kinds with one person. And now it seems possible that that love is the only thing that will outlive us all, but only if we continue to tell its story.

■ ■ ■

I don't remember the day my father died. I don't remember Lishie standing at the clothesline when the soldier came to tell her the news. I don't remember the way she nodded her graying head, turned, went back to pinning shirts and skirts, unable to cry for a long while. I don't remember how relieved Lishie was that his body, under the circumstances, would be returned when so many others were not. I don't remember my father's face cradled in the pine casket by one of Lishie's special quilts. I don't remember any of that. Barely four months old at the time, I couldn't have. I've reconstructed images from stories and pictures and stitched them into one of Lishie's quilts.

I do not remember the paleness of the pine box as it was precariously lowered into the deep earthen hole. I do not remember Preacherman sprinkling dry specks of red clay on top, an act that later seemed terribly disrespectful to my six-year-old self when Lishie explained it to me at an aunt's funeral—an act that made me wonder if my father deserved such treatment.

I don't remember Preacherman announcing, "Dust to dust," but he must have.

Sometimes I think that I remember smells, but only when I smell them at new funerals.

Grease.

Lillies.

Tobacco.

Vanilla.

Fresh dirt.

Pine sap.

I remember one taste, though it must have just been repeated so many times after that day that I've convinced myself of it—the bitterest salt I have ever tasted—Lishie's tear when she scooped me up and held me so tightly that my open lips smashed into her cheek.

"You were his," I think I remember her saying. "You are mine," I am certain I remember her saying. Even though all of this is surely impossible.

I don't remember my uncle Bud, or rather his shadow, jutting from the doorway. But there has always been a shadow between him and me, between him and my father; so it must have been there that day.

I don't remember the many different scales of cries from many different throats.

Gun shots surely rang—must have been twenty-one, three from seven men. I seem to remember more.

Lishie wailed.

Bud shouted, garbled and wet.

Too young to even crawl, I could swear I remember running past folded arms and hiding beneath one of Lishie's special quilts until a new sun rose and all I could smell was coffee.

I awoke to find Lishie had curled herself around me, indistinguishable from her homespun patchwork.

That's the impossible memory I've crafted. No amount of time visiting Bud's house changed that.

I wonder if the bones of my father are exposed and clean now. I picture a perfect white skeleton, fully intact, framed within the pine coffin—like the one I saw in anatomy class. So perfectly preserved, the bones could teach. I know it sounds odd to speak of my father like that, but you have to understand, I never knew him in the flesh. I never felt the breath of his lungs. His memory is as much a skeleton as his body.

Yet Lishie was always present. It was as if she radiated— sometimes even radiated right through me. I remember walking in her door after I returned from junior college. I hadn't said a word and I surely hadn't made up my mind if I

I picture a perfect white skeleton, full intact, framed within the pine coffin—like the one I saw in anatomy class.

was ever going back. She looked up from where she sat in her rocking chair, sighed a heavy sigh, and let her hands fall from her quilting to rest in her lap. "Oh, Cowney," she whispered. That is all she said, but I knew she knew everything. She understood far more than even I did about how I was feeling or how I would come to feel. I knew then and there that I wasn't going back because she knew it first. She wasn't judging me or even pitying me. She just stirred within me until it was all sorted out.

Except for the valley land that began pimpling with improvised storefronts, Cherokee was not the Cherokee of today. Cherokee was of mud-chinked log cabins burrowed into mountain hollers, surprising expanses of neat garden rows jutting across rare unwooded land at the end of roughly carved dirt roads—half-washed away in the spring and summer and impassable with snow in the winter. But no matter where human life chose to carve its mark on the land, it did not stray far from water—creek, river, stream, or fall—follow one and you would find Cherokee. You would find the smoke from woodstoves. You would find red clay ground into a fine, ginger dust coating the surface of life. And you could not find it directly from any highway. To trust a road is still a road when it looks like a creek is not and has never been for the tourist's heart. Yet, it is only that trust that will get you from a road sign to a home. Or, in my case, from Lishie's where I lived, to Bud's, where I worked.

■ ■ ■

Bud's cabin was short of breath, strangled by the dust of his daily existence and by the humid draft of his lungs. He was the only man I knew whose sweat seemed to flow simultaneously from the pores of his body and the foulness of his words. I grabbed the besom from beside the front door and walked out to sweep the porch.

"I guess you're glad you're a gimp, for once in your life." My uncle Bud sure had a way with words. "Weren't for that skee-jawed foot of yours, you'd be knee-deep in Nazis." He tossed a tattered, two-day old newspaper onto a pile, a collection of three months' worth of international posturing and local weather reports, each paper a near carbon copy of the one that lay beneath it.

I shrugged. He wasn't asking a question. He never really asked questions.

"You can thank your momma for that. She was in too big of a hurry to get you out."

He reminded me of this often.

I grunted, so the words forming on my tongue couldn't slip through my lips. These were not debates. Not even arguments. Bud was Bud and my only purpose, in his mind, was to be an echo in his presence. If I had cared more about him, I might've tried to offer my opinion once in a while. But I found it no real victory to earn him as an ally, so I echoed. He was a cavern whose hollow center managed to trap errant winds. I drank his vibrations. Still, he was mostly right. Since birth, the bones of my left foot have conspired against my body's natural compass and collectively pointed outward, tempting me to lead my life in circles.

"Better a penguin than a pigeon," my mother was said to have remarked when the midwife laid me in her arms. They both knew then that the foot would never fully correct itself. The midwife had seen too many births and she recounted all similar situations to everyone in attendance. My mother prayed for a "remarkable son." She confessed it to the midwife as if she signed a legal contract with God. These were the stories I was told from Lishie, not Bud.

Perhaps my foot could have been corrected, but the week following my birth was spent trying to save my mother's life rather than tend to the non-essentials of me. Deep down I still felt that urgency to protect my mother as Bud placed his irresponsible blame, but I just echoed.

"I reckon 'bout all your cousins are over yonder now. You best believe that means you've got twice the work to do 'round here. Uncle Sam may let you off the hook, but you're going to need more than a twisted flipper to just lay up here all summer. We got a lot of work to tend to 'fore harvest."

"Or before I leave for school."

"Yeah, I'm not holding my breath for that one."

Bud always spoke like I had shied from work, that I had refused to cut and hang tobacco or hoe the tater garden or milk old Bess. My disabled foot translated to disabled resolve in his book. The only work he recognized as *work* was within his gaze. I would spend hours, over-time even, at the inn, but he couldn't attest to my efforts. So it was as if I was on some sort of holiday while he waited at home listing the chores in preparation for my return. He certainly didn't think doing my schoolwork was praiseworthy. This led me to stop altogether when I was with him. Lishie didn't seem to mind me reading or doing arithmetic at the table. I think she might've even liked it. She said my mother used to write poetry—though I've never seen any trace of it.

"I'll tell you one thing. Back in my day, you'd have to have more than just one gimp limb to keep you from shippin' off to fight for your country." Bud punctuated his statement with the ping of the spittoon. He rubbed his knees, acknowledging his gout flair-ups he blamed on old war injuries. Again, no proof of that.

I rolled my eyes, but kept my head down so he wouldn't launch into the long version of his tired lecture.

"Hell. If it wasn't for guys like me and your dad, this wouldn't even be your country." And again, Bud was only half right. All Indians were finally recognized as U.S. citizens following WWI partially because of the service of so many volunteers like Bud and my father; but I was fairly certain it would have happened without Bud's contribution. The only letter sent home that ever arrived from my father mentioning

Bud's service insinuated that Bud spent more time trying not to get kicked out of the infirmary than he did working a post. Lishie used to show me the letter when I got sad. Still, Bud and his brother *had* volunteered, even when they were told that they would not be conscripted. Lishie always said it was because they liked to fight and it didn't matter who or for whom. I think it also had something to do with not having a job. The war was over for all intents and purposes when they arrived in Europe.

Outside Bud's cabin, the black-capped Chickadee whistled a lonesome song, piercing and unrequited notes. The Indigo Bunting darted between tree limbs like the woodland sprite I had once seen in a book Lishie brought home from the Goat Man peddler.

Lishie had asked a cousin in Charleston to write her when the Goat Man made his way through their city so that she might time his arrival in Cherokee. Even while exhibiting amazingly accurate travel estimation, Lishie made futile journeys to town three times before he arrived and she was able to trade a month's worth of savings from her humble mending services for the volume. The copy was well worn and two pages were completely missing, but what remained seemed magical and questionable in the context of Lishie's conservative religious practices. This was a woman who damn near burned *Ulysses* when she found it (and read nearly a quarter of it overnight) among the books I overconfidently resolved to complete before the age of twenty after my teacher, Ms. Majorie, assured me I was bright enough to do so. Joyce being "The Devil's whisperer" according to Lishie, I barely glimpsed the final pages before it was confiscated. Perhaps the Bunting-esque spirits of a fairytale were somehow godlier than man's quest for godliness.

The Indigo Bunting reminded me that the merging of forest's stillness and its interruption marked by fierce velocity was what made the woods the wilderness. Hovering just outside Hawthorne's darkness, though less judicious than Sherwood Forest, it was a wood not yet known in literature or picture shows. Now I know what you must be thinking. That all sounds starry-eyed, maybe even romantic. But that's why you need the stories of this place. No outsiders seemed to know what I knew, what we knew about these woods. Few outsiders knew the contradictions of poison oak and healing salves growing side by side, or the way in which grapevines have nothing to do with eating and so much to do with flying. And that... well, that was fine by me then. But you will need to know.

I was also one of the few who recognized old man Tsa Tsi's Capuchin monkey, Edgar, simply by the way the tree branches bent overhead. Tsa Tsi, or George (his English name), was one of those fixture characters many of us have known in our childhood. He was a man who never seemed to age nor would ever die. As a child, I was perpetually nervous in his presence, fearful he could see deep to the root of my motivations and ambitions and judge them ceaselessly without saying a word. One sideways glance by the old man and I was transformed. I never actually saw him move from one place to the other, now that I think about it. I can't recall when or how I met him or when I decided we should go on conversing like life-long friends. Of course, there were lots of folks like that back then. Formal introductions weren't needed. Just like I never introduced myself to the stream below my house or my great aunts that I saw maybe once or twice in my lifetime. Some things, some people just seem to always have existed within our own sphere of being, indefinable by common terms of friendship or familial relationship. Just people, peopling our world. And of course, I still laugh to think that such an apathetic man cared for a ridiculous monkey named Edgar. But, as a child, it all made perfect sense.

Edgar's leap caused the limbs of the forest to dip much lower than a squirrel's, though he was also far less clumsy than the local woodland flyers. He made very little noise. Tsa Tsi insisted it was because he was deaf. I wasn't so sure about that because I couldn't figure how a monkey could survive the panthers without hearing them sneak up on him. I've never heard that monkeys have a strong sense of smell. I'm pretty certain Edgar was quiet because Edgar had to be quiet. To survive. I know a little something about that.

Often, standing on the porch, even though I could not see his tiny black, brown and white body, I could see his path zigzagging back to Tsa Tsi's place over the hill. Pines bending. Oak leaves dancing. Maples swaying as if a strong gust of wind had managed to coil its way within the confines of the forest. His movement was in such congruence with the treetops I

Edgar's leap caused the limbs of the forest to dip much lower than a squirrel's, though he was also far less clumsy than the local woodland flyers.

couldn't help but feel he was naturally meant to be there.

I guess it's safe to say that the old man was the only one around who kept a monkey as a pet and the only monkey owner in the whole wide world who thought it perfectly natural to let said pet roam at will. Edgar caused more than one hunter to go into near cardiac arrest a time or two. But more folks in the area by then knew to be on the watch for him and would relay sightings to Tsa Tsi so he wouldn't worry. Not that he was prone to worrying.

A few years back, while I was up at his place helping to split wood, the old man sat on a stump rolling cigarette after cigarette, and told me about how he came to acquire

Edgar. It seems that the carnival was making its way through Cherokee one summer. Early thirties, late twenties... something like that. The carnival wasn't stopping here for a show because no one in Cherokee had any money anyway, but sometimes it would set up camp for performers to rest before moving on to another town for a week of shows. Edgar was a trained tightrope walker, wore a top hat and tiny red vest. Unfortunately, he also had a problematic tendency to lift ladies' skirts and nip at children who tried to pet him. The carnival manager kept him in a miniscule metal cage for those reasons. "Weren't fit for a 'possum," Tsa Tsi shook his head, thinking back.

Tsa Tsi told me that one day while they were in camp, he went down to see if the carnies might be interested in buying some wild greens or deer jerky. "They paid a fair price for fresh goods," he offered. He told me that the place looked pretty deserted, so he eased his way into one of the larger circus-style tents *for a look-see*. When he saw Edgar the first time, the monkey was clenching the bars of his cage and shaking the entire structure so hard that the bottom kept lifting from the ground. As Edgar saw Tsa Tsi entering the tent and approach his cage, Edgar just stopped, and as Tsa Tsi says (though who's to know what's really true), "he began to grin like a fool" at Tsa Tsi and calmed right down.

It all seems like a crazy story to me (and probably you) now, but the old man did tell me something that I took to heart. We were sitting outside the trading post on a split log bench. I sipped an RC Cola, desperate to cool off from the walk down the mountain and he, as he always did, seemed to have been sitting there his whole life.

I took a long sip as Tsa Tsi picked up the story at its midpoint.

"And right then I knew what I had to do. See, Pap used to tell me about sneaking down to the stockade and taking food to his older brother and his family right before they moved 'em west during the Removal. He used to tell me that the government had made an animal of his brother and that he knew he could never get caught or he'd become one too. So he hid out in the mountains and later stayed with a family who'd been traded a small piece of land 'cause freedom was worth more than life."

And that's why old man Tsa Tsi never left the Qualla Boundary either and how he came to end up with a Capuchin monkey named Edgar, who I'm guessing he just up and stole—because Tsa Tsi wasn't much for negotiations with white folk.

I asked him once why he'd named him Edgar. He told me that he'd named him after Edgar Allen Poe. I don't know what I think about that. Wouldn't have suspected Tsa Tsi to have even read Poe; but then again, Tsa Tsi didn't seem to fit into molds so easily.

Now, as for Edgar, he was even more adventurous than Tsa Tsi and loved to explore and that's why he nearly sent quite a few people to an early grave. Edgar had been seen as far away as Tennessee and Georgia. He always made his way back to Tsa Tsi, though. He might be gone a whole month, but he'd come ambling into Tsa Tsi's cabin, hungry as hell, no worse for the wear. So I think Tsa Tsi saw no point in keeping him tied or locked up and the rest of us got to enjoy having our very own Capuchin monkey hanging out in our woods. We didn't even have to go to a zoo for a taste of the exotic.

■ ■ ■

Ever since I could remember, I wanted to escape Cherokee and that feeling of suffocation just kept growing with my body. But just as I was about to finally get out at least for a summer, I felt as if I was rushing carelessly out of the woods, saw briers pricking my bare forearms and legs, leaving trickles of blood to mix with the sweat of haste. I started thinking of all of the things I would miss like ripe berries left on the bush. Lishie's hand over her mouth when she got tickled. The way a cool mist rises from the Oconaluftee as if sighing at the rising sun. The chattering of the Indigo Buntings. And a place where a monkey could scamper across oak and maple limbs like a tightrope performer. If I thought too much about the sweetness of my place in the world, I might never be able to leave it. ■

AN EXCERPT FROM

CRAZY HOUSE

ANNIE FRAZIER

I'll *have* that little man.

That's what Mama said to me the first time she caught sight of Bill, standing there in a grubby Food Lion in North Raleigh, overripe fruit smells wafting all around. I hefted a jug of laundry detergent into the cart and turned to look and there Bill was. Price-checking dish soap, getting up real close to the tags to see the difference per ounce. He went with the store brand, nodded, lifted his chin and saw us.

First glance, Bill looked raggedy-ass to me. Not the greatest head of hair but not bald either—close-cropped, fuzzy, color of damp sand where it wasn't gray. Looked like his styling technique involved rubbing both palms hard against his scalp. Pleated chinos two sizes too big, Hawaiian-print polo shirt apparently tucked in *after* he'd cinched his belt down tight, aviator-style glasses magnifying his eyes. Bright green eyes, though. Green like moss after rain.

Rough as Bill looked to me, I guess Mama saw potential. A project, maybe. She saw a compact man, jaw square and sharp as a table edge. She saw that he might look almost refined if you coaxed him out of the pleats and the palm frond patterns and the glasses like chem-lab safety goggles, if you found him some clothes that fit. She cleared her throat, sucked her flat belly concave and pushed her tits out. All to Bill's apparent delight.

Hello ladies, he said. Dipped his head an inch, like tipping a top hat. Mama shifted weight onto her left hip. To make it jut, make her waist bend.

Well hello there, she said. *Where* did you find that festive shirt?

Bill said, Oh I got this one visiting family down in Florida. He stared down the front of it as if he needed to double check that he'd referenced the right one.

They introduced themselves and Mama made her voice go whispery to say he looked *mighty* handsome in that shirt. Said it even though it did him no favors. He blushed, staring right into her cleavage squeezed up nearly to her chin.

Mama always made a habit of flinging out breathy compliments much too soon, which I'm sure had everything to do with the caliber of boyfriend she'd brought home all those years. Did it like a nervous tic, like if she didn't start the flow of compliments immediately there'd be none flowing back to her.

Bill stuttered out something about her perfume smelling like cookies and Mama sidled closer, brushed her fingers against his arm and said, Well aren't you sweet. Vanilla's my favorite scent.

I may as well have been a hundred miles away. Rest of the world a blur to them, it seemed. Standing on the outside, I sensed the electricity. Not the dangerous kind that'll sting you, though. The dreamy kind makes even grown folks stare and grin and giggle.

Bill did finally notice I was there. Looked over at my sixteen-year-old self and asked if Mama and I were sisters. She squealed and I rolled my eyes way up in my head, unable to abide that tired old line again.

We are not, I said.

Mama stepped back and elbowed me and whispered, You better quit that.

So I quit it and smiled real sweet at yet another strange man about to attempt the troubling calculus required to figure Mama and me out. I knew what to expect. It'd been the same routine for years. Dude sizing Mama up, the angles and curves of her. Levi's 512s like a vice grip, same ones she'd worn for twenty years. Hair bleached near-white, teased up and set crunchy, face all symmetry and openness and light and spider-heavy mascara. Dude looking over at me in my tank top and man-sized flannel shirt and black jeans and green Doc Martens with the laces frayed, looking at my dark hair hanging long, my molars clenched down hard and fierce, eyes staring deadly right through him. Then—the best part—dude looking squint-eyed back at Mama, his face a series of questions.

A conundrum. That's what we've presented to new folks ever since eighth grade when my body reshaped itself in Mama's image but I refused to follow suit in any other department.

And yet, Bill didn't look at us like the rest. More like he was trying *not* to look. He didn't even squint back at Mama at the end, just smiled and stuck his hand out toward me and said, I'm Bill. And you are? I shook his hand, said my name, felt myself soften without meaning to. Tried to regain some kind of edge by setting my jaw again, but couldn't ignore the flitting thought that such a softening might very well mean something. I let the thought go, decided to play it cool until I saw whether Mama went for him in earnest.

Not ten minutes later, those two paraded out the sliding doors with parallel carts into the stagnant heat of mid-August, phone numbers scribbled in spaces between receipt-back carwash coupons. I brought up the rear, scuffing my heels on the asphalt all the way to the car, wondering what in hell had just happened.

They made eyes, promised to call, parted ways.

Mama hummed all the way home with the windows down, warm breeze on our faces. Took me a while to place it, but then I realized she was humming Dolly's "Green Eyed Boy." Oh the sigh I let out. *Mama that's a sad song*, I thought. *Don't jump to that part yet.* But jumping two-footed is the only way Mama's ever known to do things. Every new man she met, she'd start off humming some old Dolly song. But always, eventually, there she'd be playing "Jolene" on repeat when things fell apart.

She hummed the sad song happy, I guess because it fit Bill on the surface—the green eyes part, not the boy part. Hummed it like she loved looking into that green, letting herself fall way down in it. She wholly ignored the many melancholy words about lost love, about regret. How like Mama—forever cutting those gray eyes away from anything unpleasant.

I shook my head and turned on the radio. Dixie Chicks singing "Ready to Run."

Goddamnit, I thought, *not this either.*

I spun the sound way down, took a breath and prepared myself for the inevitable—me watching Mama fall for another one, then swooping in a few weeks or months later to pick up the pieces of her sweet broken heart, holding onto her and saying yet again, Mama it's gonna be alright. We're gonna be alright.

But that's not what happened at all. After years of misfires, Mama finally hit the target she'd been aiming at. Waltzed into that Food Lion, filled her shopping cart, marched out with a bonus future husband in tow.

■ ■ ■

Wasn't the first time her life changed in a grocery store, either. April Fool's Day of 1985—just a couple weeks shy of her eighteenth birthday, Mama's water broke a month early, mid-shift at the Piggly-Wiggly up in Creedmoor. She scanned the barcode on some old man's honey ham and then—*whoosh.* Late morning sunlight glinting off the puddle at her feet, man looking away, gagging and fanning himself with a thick stack of rumpled fives and ones.

Just two hours later, I shot wailing into the blinding lights of the maternity ward at Rex Hospital in Raleigh. Tiny thing, red as a skinned squirrel in the photos, Mama's eyes wide and her mouth a hard line looking down at me, just a scrunched squalling thing balanced in the crook of her arm.

She'd gotten pregnant the summer before her senior year of high school, dropped out because she didn't want the world to see the former head cheerleader big as a house, lumbering through the halls. Also because when her mother Jane found out, she kicked Mama out. Which meant that working enough hours to afford Spaghetti-Os and Pampers became more immediately crucial to her than retaking Algebra II or memorizing the military history of our great nation.

Mama's grandmother, Grammy, had given up on her daughter Jane years before and gladly took in my child-mother. Helped raise me. Grammy was seventy-nine when I arrived, yet there's a whole pile of pictures of her tending to me in those early days like some young grandma. She's patting my ruddy infant back to burp me, wiping Gerber mush out of my white wispy hair, hooking a finger over the back of my diaper to check its contents and frowning at what she's found.

I've never known my father. Abiding truth of my life though it may be, it's still a hard thing to think about with any clarity. Always sounds like an admission of guilt, even in my own head. Mama told me she tried to get him involved. Showed him the stick she'd peed on, went right along with it when he said they

There may have been a span of time when I didn't yet realize I'd been missing a daddy, but I don't recall the feeling.

ought to name me Krystal because he'd been to a Krystal Burger outside Knoxville once and thought it looked cool spelled like that. Named me after goddamn steamed miniature hamburgers and then took off the minute Mama started to show.

Hoping he might come back but figuring he wouldn't, Mama told the lady in the hospital to write down Krystal Elizabeth Robinson on all my forms. Smart move, giving me her own last name. She borrowed my middle name from Grammy, who had the further wisdom to suggest they go ahead and call me Lizzie instead of Krystal.

There may have been a span of time when I didn't yet realize I'd been missing a daddy, but I don't recall the feeling. I *do* have a hazy memory of asking Mama why the other kids at daycare got to have daddies. She made this sad whimpery noise in her throat, pulled me on her lap and tucked my head under her chin. Didn't say anything for a while. But how do you explain to a three-year-old that her teenage daddy ran away once things stopped being fun? You don't. Or at least Mama didn't. All she said was, Baby I don't know.

It became her mantra whenever I asked about him.

Where's my daddy?

Baby I don't know.

What's my daddy like?

Baby I don't know.

Mama eventually got clever, told me I should make up my own story about where he'd disappeared to. I took to that idea real fast. First I made him an astronaut on a mission to Mars. His rocket ship had broken but what he did all day in that lonely red desert was carve *Burdy and Lizzie* into giant alien rocks and devise outlandish plans to get himself home. Then I made him a treasure hunter, lost in a faraway land like in my favorite book—all exotic plants and dangerous animals with gnashing teeth and sharp claws. A place there was little chance he'd ever escape but *gosh* I could always hope.

All sorts of stories filled my mind about where that man was, not one of them remotely close to the truth.

■ ■ ■

I was brutally skeptical of Bill to begin with, partly because Mama and I were still on pretty shaky ground with each other right then, but also because I'd learned long before to be the questioning force in all her relationships. She'd sure never borne that burden herself.

But Bill turned out to be a different kind of man than I'd ever been around. The kind of man sits in his car to update his checkbook register before driving home to put the groceries away. Kind of man reads Ann Landers and Dear Abby for his own personal edification. Frugal man, but generous. Kind of man willing to unhinge his chest and bare his beating heart from day one, willing to help provide for us because it makes that heart beat stronger in him, willing to help me pay for Duke when I'd been crossing my fingers that I'd be able to afford community college.

Bill's also the kind of man who—six months before the wedding, seven months before freshman move-in day—hardly blinks when he learns that Mama's got thirty-grand owed across eight credit cards. Debts she'd kept secret from the world, including me. All eight of those cards paid minimum each month, Mama scribbling checks late at night at the kitchen counter, me asleep and dreaming. Unaware.

Bill's the kind of man says, New plan. Let's wait to buy a house. Let's work on that debt and get Lizzie started at school and reassess in a couple years. In the interim I'll quit renting and move in here. If you'll have me.

Kind of man pats the back of Mama's shaky hand while she nods a wordless answer. Kind of man looks solemn at the worry etched across my face and says, Don't you dare think of it Lizzie. Says it before I can even open my mouth to apologize for what I'm costing him. Sees my eyes fill up and says, Sweetheart don't you know by now that I'd rather help you pay for college and help your mother clear this debt than buy some silly house?

Yes Bill. I know.

■ ■ ■

By *move in here*, Bill meant our double-wide out on what's left of the old family farm, where I've lived my whole life. Mama drilled it into my head early and often to be proud of what we had. Grateful too, since the trailer was Grammy's and we were her guests until the summer after I turned five. That's when she made use of her stocks and bonds and careful savings, bought an apartment at the old folks home. Springmoor, name full of youth and hope, place where Grammy could hop on her new Jazzy scooter and blow through the halls to play bridge.

The trailer sits pressed up against woods, just the width of the dirt driveway between it and the farmhouse Grammy grew up in. She lived in that farmhouse until the mid-seventies when its needs became more than she could handle on her own. Her siblings had all passed by then, Grammy being the family's surprise child, born a decade after the last of the main herd. Imagine—six brothers and sisters born in the nineteenth century, and you the modern girl born five years into the twentieth.

As a last-ditch effort, she offered the house to her daughter Jane, Mama's mama. But Jane was too full of spite to care about anything but her many grudges. One of which was her smoldering anger that Grammy openly hated Jane's no-good, gambling, violent husband Bo. Jane couldn't even think clear enough to realize Grammy was offering a free house so Jane and Bo and Mama and Mama's little sister Sandy could finally move out of the musty apartment they'd been in for a decade. But Bo wouldn't have it, so Jane wouldn't have it.

Mama's daddy was about as bad as they come, from what I've heard all my life. I guess Grammy once had real high hopes for her darling daughter Jane. Hopes that didn't include Jane taking up with a guy whose idea of a fun Friday night was driving around with a cooler full of cheap beer in the truck bed, steering one-fingered with his left elbow propped in the open window, his right hand squeezed down between Jane's thighs. And Jane just gazing at him like a fool.

Or at least that's how Mama said Grammy used to tell it. I assume Grammy wasn't there for any of those joy rides, though, so the accuracy of her detailed description seems dubious.

■ ■ ■

Mama didn't talk much about her parents until Bill first came around. Then she opened up like a big old flower, sharing bits and pieces I'd never heard before.

Once Mama said, I guess my daddy was a real fun party boy back when he and my mama dated. They eloped when they were sixteen. Had to drive down to South Carolina where you could get married that young without a note from your parents. After I was born my daddy quit being able to hold down a job more than a few months at a time. Gambled away every penny he could get his hands on. The drunker he was the more he pushed my mother around. Slamming her into the kitchen counters. Bruising up her hips.

Bill shook his head and closed his eyes.

He pushed me and Sandy around too, Mama said. Over the years my mama got more and more resentful of her life but she refused to believe my daddy was the problem. Took his side whenever he got rough with me and Sandy. Just stood there smoking a Virginia Slim real aggressive, telling Sandy and me what little shits we both were.

Mama mimicked her mother smoking— hunch-shouldered, cheeks sucked way in, lips puckered, distinct tremor in that smoking hand.

I knew the rest of the story. Knew that when Mama got knocked up and kicked out, Grammy was glad to take her in, but wished she could've gotten ahold of Sandy too. Grammy told me once she couldn't bear thinking of little Sandy alone in that house with that monster of a daddy, but there just wasn't much she could do. I guess if you're a mama and grandmama who's taking in kids but still trying to be polite, and if your aim is not to get your daughter beat up or worse, you can only go so far.

Still. It never seemed fair to me that Mama got out and Sandy didn't. But I guess that's why Sandy scooted her skinny ass across the whole expanse of the country the minute she finished high school. Made a home for herself in Seattle far from anyone she'd ever known.

Faced with all that—daughter refusing a generous offer, house fixing to fall down around her—Grammy finally bought the trailer. Had the delivery man park it where she could keep one watchful eye on the old home place, its once-blue paint fading to gray, floorboards of the huge wraparound porch sagging closer to the ground each year. A couple of upstairs windows still had curtains in them, gauzy in their gradual disintegration. In a stiff breeze, they moved just enough to give the impression of the house blinking.

■ ■ ■

Could've been a scary place to grow up next to, I guess, but it never did bother me. Grammy showed me old pictures of the place that made it seem like a grand and ancient monument to the lives of my ancestors. I can see those hazy black-and-whites so clear, without even needing to dig them out of Grammy's old shoebox of jumbled tiny photos. One in particular feels like a memory—like I was there for its making. In it you see the farmhouse head-on. The oaks to the left were smaller then, but they already rose almost to the roof, casting shade on the house and the yard and on Grammy's parents rocking on the porch—four ghost-white eyes peering out, two pale paper fans blurring through the long exposure.

First time I saw that one, Grammy held the picture between thumb and forefinger right at the corner and said, That porch was the coolest place in Raleigh on a summer afternoon. We didn't have air conditioning back then you know. Just had to sit out there waiting for the breeze to come.

They were farmers and most of the original forty-some acres of land were planted in alfalfa and corn and tomatoes. Grammy's mother cooked a giant breakfast every morning for the whole family. The men and boys would fill up on sausage and big biscuits and eggs just laid by the chickens in the yard, then go work in the fields all day. Come in at dusk all dark and dirty, the glow of sweat on their skin. They planted in spring, harvested all summer, canned in the fall and waited out the winter, year after year. Feels special, living and walking on the same ground where my people've lived and walked since way back. Different world, same ground.

■ ■ ■

Before kindergarten started, it seemed to me that we had it all—clean comfortable home, fridge and pantry full of food, Mama and Grammy loving on me all the time. And we did, in that regard. But when school started, I got glimpses of what we lacked, felt the sting of kids mobbing together, turning on me, picking apart the differences.

No matter what, though, Mama's always been unwaveringly proud of that double-wide. Proud of how tidy she kept it, how good it always looked. When I was three, she worked out a deal with her handy boyfriend Jason to fix it up. He put in snap-together wood floors and replaced the standard issue shiny linoleum in the kitchen and bathrooms. Still linoleum, but the good kind. Grammy got into it and declared that she wanted something real snazzy for the kitchen floor, picked out those black-and-white checkerboard tiles you see in old diners.

Jason's biggest accomplishment, though, was the front porch. Built it deep and wide enough to hold four long beach chairs, the kind that flop flat so you can nap on them like a cot. He stained the porch dark and added flourish with beveled railings and built-in flower boxes.

A tall man, Jason. So tall he had to duck going through doorways to keep his hair from brushing against the jamb. He'd swoop me up and set me on his bony shoulders and we'd walk out through the back field, Mama beside us with one hand clutched tight in his, blade of grass pressed between his lips bobbing with every step.

Sweet as he'd been, Jason finished renovating and promptly realized he wasn't yet interested in family life. He and Mama weren't but twenty-one, so I suppose you can't blame him too much. Still, I'm sure it was a hard thing for Mama—second man in a row to walk away from her. I watched her cry day after day, sitting hunched and cross-legged on one of the porch beach chairs. All I knew to do was climb into the scoop of her lap, rest my cheek on her shoulder and say, Mama don't cry.

■ ■ ■

One Saturday morning, probably fed up with Mama's lengthy breakup funk, Grammy marched out of her bedroom and flipped off the cartoons we'd been watching. She said, I've got an idea. Let's put in a salad garden. Need to get it done this weekend or it'll be too late.

Dogwoods were blooming, so I guess I'd just turned four.

We piled in Grammy's car and rode up to the Southern States in Creedmoor to get supplies—two-by-sixes, seeds, bagged-up mix of soil and composted manure to darken and soften the red clay we had to work with.

A couple blocks of low glass-front brick buildings line both sides of Main Street in Creedmoor, then after another block or two, town and Main Street both end abruptly at a Y-intersection. Back then Southern States sat nestled into the crotch between roads—big old whitewashed building, wood siding, grey shingled roof.

We walked in and I was struck by the sweet dusty smell of the place, the high ceiling with its exposed beams criss-crossing so far above me that they blurred behind atmospheric haze, floorboards worn smooth and shiny underfoot by decades of scuffing work boots.

I heard a nervous whispery *cheep-cheep* and followed it until I found baby chicks bumping against each other by the

I watched the chicks, mesmerized, wanting to reach and gather them chirping and flapping in my arms, but I knew not to...

dozen at the bottom of galvanized tubs, downy yellow feathers fluffed up, tiny clawed feet just barely crunching pine bedding, heat lamps clamped to the tubs casting warm red puddles in one corner of the dim room.

I watched the chicks, mesmerized, wanting to reach and gather them chirping and flapping in my arms, but I knew not to, knew I couldn't be gentle enough. Even now, I feel that lofty building all around my little self, smell the unfamiliar feed and farm aromas, see those baby chicks so soft and delicate and disoriented. I feel the wanting of them, the ache of restraint.

Mama and Grammy dug and planted our new garden right across the driveway, at the back corner of the farmhouse. They both got serious about growing things, tending to the garden they'd made together, babying the vegetables and the flowers equally. Flowers everywhere, too—in the boxes on the porch rail, in beds running the front length of the trailer, in cracking terra cotta pots over by the old house, in baskets hanging from anything that would hold them, some even swinging from oak and poplar branches.

Tomatoes and squash and sometimes a watermelon or two grew each summer in our little garden. Got to where Grammy's knees and back hurt her if she did the bending and stooping and reaching required, so Mama gradually took over the bulk of the work. On weekend mornings she'd toss her hair up in a rough ponytail with loose pieces curling down the back of her neck, slip on her big movie star sunglasses and proceed to spend hours weeding and pruning and watering, teaching me the same things Grammy had once taught her.

I especially liked it when Mama talked to the plants, as if they'd grow and bloom and fruit without the expense of fertilizer if she encouraged them sweet enough. She even sang to them sometimes, her voice soft and high. I thought if I were a plant I sure would try extra hard for her.

■ ■ ■

One muggy Sunday morning right before Grammy moved, she and Mama showed me how to sucker a tomato plant, pinching off the little shoots sent out between bigger stalks. Grammy stood watching us with a hand on her hip.

Mama said, If you don't pluck the suckers all the energy goes to making leaves instead of tomatoes. Isn't that right Grammy?

Grammy nodded and said, Mm-hm.

Mama said, Now Mr. Tomato Plant I'm gonna get this sucker real quick. Just a little pinch. There you go.

I tried a few, Mama's hands guiding mine. Grammy standing a few feet away smiling down on me. Both women saying what a good job I had done. I sniffed at my fingers the whole rest of the day, breathing in that earthy green tomato stalk smell, so proud of what I'd learned.

■ ■ ■

Mama was just thirty-four when we met Bill. He was fifty-two. And I was sixteen. He'd recently retired from a twenty-five-year career out in Research Triangle Park, doing computer-oriented work I still don't fully understand. Something with coding. Algorithms. He still tries to explain sometimes but he gets bogged down in technical jargon and my eyes glaze over, hard as I try to stop them.

In that quarter century of work he made a comfortable pile of money, always saved more than he spent, nested it up and sat on it like a mama bird. Things got dicey for a minute during his divorce, but the law came down on his side, saved him from the financial ruin his first wife GeorgeAnn had hoped for him. Just two years after their wedding.

What Bill didn't avoid was the personal ruin, the heartbreak that kept him living alone in a bare beige apartment in North Raleigh for five years storing up his paychecks and investing wisely. Going with the Food Lion store brand every damn time. Losing all the pounds old GeorgeAnn had packed on him with her starchy cooking, until all his clothes fit floppy on him.

And then he met us.

When Mama stumbled into him tits first, she inadvertently shone a light on all his darkness. Lit him right up. From day one Bill found my crazy-ass mother fascinating. Her big blonde hair and big fake nails but mostly her big loving heart, her infectious enthusiasm.

84

Those first months with him, Mama stayed fired up. Always ready to go and do.

Let's go out and do something Billy. I just wanna go *do* something, she'd say.

Said it pressed up tight to him, red acrylics tickling his chin, one thigh lodged between his legs, Bill going all pink in the face with his eyes roving the house in search of anything to land on but me.

I wanted to say, Seen it before Billy.

But I never wanted to break his heart so I'd just keep my head down and let him ever-so-gingerly peel Mama off him, readjust his glasses and say, Where to Miss Burdy?

They'd hop in his white Volvo—in impeccable shape even at the ripe old age of twelve—and ride toward town for lunch. Or he'd take her to Stuff 'n' Such, her favorite store, bright shiny knick-knacks forever jam-packed from floor to ceiling, scents of a thousand different candles mingled together so strong it made your eyes water to walk in. He'd buy her something little just to watch her clap her pretty hands together, hear those stacked bracelets clank and jingle.

■ ■ ■

Bill took an immediate liking to me. Unnerved, I gave him considerable heat, tried to push him far far away. Wasn't about to let myself get into a third shitty situation, grown man reaching and pawing at a child. But once I realized Bill was entirely different from the previous couple dudes, wasn't the least bit interested in smacking my ass or worse, I cooled off and watched him desperately attempt to be a father figure. Surprised me when he did a damn good job of it.

The generosity he offered right off the bat still boggles the mind. I'd been sitting alone under the blinking lights of the school library to type up my hand-written paper drafts the first couple years of high school, so Bill gave me a boxy gray laptop to celebrate the beginning of my senior year. Wrapped the box himself, paper loose and askew, one side taped down with the green plaid tag at the end of the Scotch roll still attached. He went on and on about what a revelation Windows 2000 would be.

Not long after that, he said he'd help with a down payment on a used car if I'd make monthly payments with my earnings from my gig as waffle cone artist at the Cow and Bucket Creamery. Bill took me car shopping and we found an '82 Volvo 240, bright red like a ripe strawberry.

These things are tanks, he said. We want you as safe as can be.

I love that damn car, that series of rectangles stuck together.

I sold for parts the Sentra Mama'd paid too much for. Old green clunker, back bumper duct taped on, front axle replaced after the original broke and sent me careening into a ditch just three weeks after Mama bought the damn thing to apologize after yet another boyfriend of hers angled for me, laid hands on me while she wasn't looking.

I still smile to imagine that car torn apart, crushed, melted down.

Pretty quick, Bill started to seem like a fairy godmother. One who snorted when he laughed and insisted on explaining the inner workings of computers in terms I couldn't wrap my mind around. But I listened anyway, in awe of his ability and willingness to sweep into our lives, picking up the slack and some of the broken pieces too.

■ ■ ■

Saturday in early October, us three bumming around the trailer, Bill proceeded to change my whole world. He asked if I had college plans and I said, I'm aiming to be a teacher. I'll see about community colleges. Wake Tech probably. Someplace that won't leave me eating Ramen for the rest of my life.

Bill nodded slow and said, I knew a kid in college who ate nothing but dried Ramen for an entire school year. He went home for the summer feeling crappy and his doctor diagnosed him with scurvy.

Scurvy?

Oh yes. So we need to avoid the all-Ramen diet for you at all cost, he said. He chuckled and slapped his knee. When he finished laughing at himself, he stood.

Alright girls. I'm going to get some paperwork done. You two relax.

Mama and I put our hair up and headed out front to pick the few straggler cherry tomatoes clinging to the vines.

He and Mama were newly engaged and he'd all but moved in with us, both developments I had tried objecting to on principle, but I came up short on hard-enough evidence to truly question the arrangement. I was as crazy for Bill as Mama was. As crazy as he was for us.

Apparently satisfied with my college ambitions, Bill hitched his pants up and disappeared into Mama's bedroom, where he'd stashed a box of recent bank statements and dividend reports and tax returns.

We were having a heat wave, heat like July almost. Sky cloudless and pale blue, sun a white-hot ball beaming down on us. Utterly relentless. Mama and I put our hair up and headed out front to pick the last few straggler cherry tomatoes clinging to the vines. We grabbed at weeds as we went and gathered about five little tomatoes in a bowl.

May as well eat these now, Mama said.

Works for me.

I plucked a big basil leaf and wrapped it around one tomato and Mama said, Ooh lemme get a couple of those.

Still chewing, she grabbed up the pile of weeds we'd made and walked across the dirt driveway to toss them at the base of a scraggly pine.

Eventual fertilizer, she said, swiping her palms against each other.

I went inside and poured two tall glasses of tea from the pitcher in the fridge and we sat sipping on the porch, sun on our bare legs, tea glasses sweating and us sweating too until the sun finally fell behind the house and Mama said, Lord baby look at the time. Let's go see what we can fix for dinner.

Bill emerged from the bedroom to find our two heads stuck in the fridge. He cleared his throat and we both jumped, knocking skulls. Mama and I each patted palm to scalp in unison and when we caught sight of each other we erupted into giggles.

Look at us, Mama said.

Hey can you rub your stomach at the same time? I asked.

Hell no, she said. She tried anyway and ended up smacking the soft part of her lower belly, which sent her into a folded-over guffaw, which in turn sent her ass crashing into a cabinet. We laughed until we made no sound.

Bill cleared his throat again and said, If I didn't know any better I might think I'd wandered into a crazy house. You two are wild tonight.

Mama said, Billy baby you *did* wander into a crazy house.

Okay ladies, Bill said. I want to talk to you both about something. I've been doing some calculating in there and I'm pleased to report that if you'll apply for as many scholarships as you can find I'll probably be able to cover what's left. But I want you to set your sights high.

I stared at him until he said, For college. At worst you'll need a small loan.

Mama and I went right on staring at him until he nodded the nod that means he's said his final word on a generous offer. Mama began boohooing, jumping up and down. I dove to hug him saying, Thank you thank you thank you.

All this before they were even married. Engaged, but still.

■ ■ ■

They had the wedding the following summer, just before I headed off to Duke. Mama's dress was cotton candy pink and a little puffier than was probably advisable but my god she looked good. Approaching elegant, somehow. True to our life together, Mama had me be her maid of honor and give her away.

When she asked me she said, Baby I need your blessing to bring Billy into our little family for good. I know I've not got the best track record but they say sometimes you just know. I never believed that until I met Bill.

She looked me in the eye—searching, hopeful, maybe a little afraid.

Mama y'all *have* my blessing, I said. You've had it a while now.

And it wasn't because Bill paid for stuff. It was because I could tell how strong he believed that we'd all three had it hard in our own ways, that we deserved something new, deserved the family we were trying so hard to become.

So there I was, balancing on that cliff that is the end of childhood, suddenly with something approximating a daddy. ■

AN EXCERPT FROM

HILLBILLY HUSTLE

WESLEY BROWNE

Knox Thompson first crossed paths with the man who would ruin him at a poker game above the arcade in downtown McKee, a forsaken place he had made it a point to avoid. After finding out about the game from one of his Porthos regulars, Knox couldn't resist. It was said to be frequented by a herd of donkeys spilling money, and that proved to be true, but making money and keeping it aren't the same thing. Especially not in Jackson County.

He knew better than to go to that sketchy-ass game, but by mid-2011 the poker boom of the aughts had cooled, online poker was illegal in the United States, and most of the good live games had dried up. At the apex, he had his choice of games in Richmond and Berea, but when poker waned, so did his options. The worst part about it was the shittiest, most casual players were the first to give it up. They say poker lessons are expensive, and it's true. Knox tried to teach at least two nights a week if he could. He had come to rely on poker winnings to keep his pizza shop and his parents afloat.

The worsening drought made him reckless. It drove him up the narrow stairwell with puckered, peeling paint into the dense smoke of the apartment over the arcade in McKee. He had told Darla, his girlfriend, and himself that if the game wasn't on the level or if things went bad, he'd just bail out.

Making his way up, Knox didn't recognize the country music that played. The steps were shallow and about every third one sagged like it was held up by wet sponges. The apartment at the top was a studio with a table and ten chairs in the middle. Off to the side was a kitchen with appliances as old as he was and a sink full of dirty dishes. A feeble folding table teetered under the weight of two Cherry Master video–slot machines. The poker table, which appeared to be from an old dining-room suite, had green felt over the top and stapled tight to the undersides. It was ringed by men, sitting in mismatched chairs that looked to have come from ten different grannies' kitchens. They wore dull flannel or black t-shirts, jeans, and boots or high-top shoes, and most were stoking cigarette cherries or had tobacco spit cups or bottles alongside. The smoke in the room was thick as white gravy but the smell of damp still pierced through. Only one person was vaping. It hadn't fully grabbed hold in Jackson County just yet.

There was one woman at the table, heavyset, wearing glasses and a faded denim shirt. She appeared to be neither smoking nor dipping. She had a half-full twenty-ounce bottle of electric-blue Mountain Dew game fuel and an open bag of Funyuns on the table beside her.

Once Knox cleared the landing, all eyes lighted on him, like a strange car passing down a country road. They had no way of knowing what he was: a guy who had built his game reading and rereading dozens of poker books, and playing countless hands live and online. He had worn his white Adidas slides with white socks—one with a Nike logo and the other without—loose mesh shorts, and a threadbare, powder-blue "Trampled by Turtles" t-shirt. He had one tattoo, a full-sleeve of fighting robots in grayscale. The most he'd done all day to his receding, curly black hair and sloppy beard was run his fingers through them. If he had any tells at all, he made sure his appearance wasn't one of them.

The table went back to the hand playing out. It ended with a bet followed by folds and a burr-headed fat kid with a chinstrap beard and diamond-looking stud earrings raking a small pile of chips and adding them to his stack all while dragging from a stubby fag. He couldn't have been more than twenty-five.

A little fellow with painstakingly combed slick dark hair who sat at the head of the table opposite the stairwell raised his chin and looked over the others. "What can we do for you?"

If Knox were smart, and listened to his better inclinations and laboring lungs, he would've said, "Nothing," and walked right back out. Being obstinate—as was his way—he said, "Sidney Fulks told me there's a hold 'em game I could play here."

"He told you right. Games 2/4 cash and they's a fifty-dollar minimum buy-in. You can buy back for less. Grab you a chair."

The man pointed at the two open seats opposite each other about midtable. Behind the little fellow stood a hulking man with his arms crossed. He had pale hair, eyebrows, and mutton chops, and a dip the size of a mouse tucked behind his lip. His veiny, thick arms were tattooed in countless flying bats. Wherever the gym was in McKee, he had put in his time plus someone else's.

Knox read the little guy as the table boss in more ways than one, so he took the open seat three to his left so he could play behind him. The chip stacks on the table ranged from around twenty dollars to somewhere around five hundred. The little guy lorded over one of the tall stacks. Knox's rule of thumb was always to buy-in for fifty times the big blind, so he peeled off two hundred in loose twenties, laid them on the table to get changed for chips, and was off.

The deal made its way around the table, each player dealing in turn. If Knox had caught any kind of hand he would've played it, but was content to fold his two hole cards and watch the action for a couple table rotations. He quickly found out the game's reputation was accurate, and his instincts were, too. The play was loose as hell and the little guy bullied and stole every stray pot nobody seemed too attached to. One time the chubby boy with the chinstrap bowed up in a small pot in which Knox strongly suspected he had a real hand, and the little fellow must have suspected it too, because after a long deliberation, he laid down what Knox felt certain was a pair of rags.

Like every new poker game Knox had ever played, he eventually got asked who he was and where he'd come from. He was an interloper amongst a lot of regulars, that was clear. He told them he owned Porthos Pizza, which led one player at the table to recollect going there while he was on a bender in Richmond.

The first pot Knox raised to twelve dollars preflop someone piped up. "What do you know. The carpetbagger's playing him a hand. Look out." He was right. Knox had been dealt jacks, which he always hated to play because they got vulnerable quick, but it was still a good hand. He wasn't the only one at the table who was judicious in his hand selection, but there were damn few. Several of the players would at least call the big blind to get a look at the initial flop if given the chance, which suited Knox. Pot sweetener in a cash game was hardly ever a bad thing.

With jacks, so long as no ace, king, or queen came on the flop, and no flush or straight seemed likely, Knox was in good shape if he didn't have too many callers. Jacks were a hand he generally preferred to play without much competition. At

The play was loose as hell and the little guy bullied and stole every stray pot nobody seemed too attached to.

twelve bucks he got three calls, including one from the little fellow, which was two more than he wanted. The flop rolled off 10, 8, 9 of different suits, good for Knox's hand. No over-cards and he picked up an open-ended straight draw. A flush hitting wasn't too likely for anyone. If nobody sat on pocket 8s, 9s, or 10s, or jack/queen, Knox was healthy. Still, he decided to push a nice size continuation bet and end the thing right there. The little guy acted first. He checked, followed by the next two. Knox counted the pot at thirty-eight dollars, so he bet thirty-five and got ready to rake it all back in.

The little fellow drew from his smoke. Then he pointed at Knox with it scissored between his fingers. "That's an awful big bet. You hit this flop? Cause I sure as hell did." Knox looked at him and smiled. He'd been to card games where he ran his mouth. In fact, he did at most, but this wasn't one to do it. Even Knox knew that.

The little guy used a small swirly slice of agate as a card protector. He slid it off, bent back his hole cards for a peek, and put it back. He spun a single chip on the felt a couple times before he stacked a full hundred in chips in front of him and pushed them to the center. After it was already out there, he said, "I raise." His check-raise was a perfectly legitimate, perfectly nasty play.

The other two players folded before he'd got the words out. Knox went back over what he thought he might have, and there was a lot that scared him. Sometimes, though, he got a tickle that said, "He ain't got it." Knox's Spidey card-sense tingled like crazy. The little guy's raise and talk seemed tailored to push him out. He called it.

When the dealer peeled the next card, the turn card, off the deck, Knox watched it right until the last. Then he sneaked a look at the little guy, who watched the card hit the table and stared it down. He didn't look at his chips, and he didn't look at Knox, just the cards in the middle. Usually, if a card was real good for a player, they didn't look at it long. They didn't want to seem too interested. It was a red seven. The second heart on the board. Knox had made a straight. The little fellow eventually glanced at his own two cards like he forgot they were there before taking Knox in again. With one more card to go, Knox was pretty sure the guy didn't have much. That was until he said, "I'm all in." The instant he said it, everything Knox was so sure of ran off with its tail tucked.

The only hand the little guy could hold that beat Knox's now was queen/jack. It was possible he could work his way to a heart flush, a full house, or even four of a kind on the last card—the river card—but at that moment, queen/jack was the only hand that bested Knox. Knox's Spidey senses now started pinging with doubt, but whenever anything like that happened, when his thoughts scattered and he lost his nerve, he went to his safe place: the math. He had learned the formulas in his poker books. He didn't have to make a hard decision, just do the math. Knox wasn't even all that good at math, but he didn't have to be perfect, just close.

While everyone watched, he peered at the chips in the middle and pointed at them as he counted. Then he counted what was left of his stack. He had only eighty-four more dollars in chips. He realized he should've pushed it all in earlier rather than just call the previous raise, but he hadn't done it. Now there was three hundred and twenty-two dollars in the pot and Knox only had to call eighty-four to win it. It was possible he was throwing good money after bad, or the little guy had flubbed it and forced him to call a bluff, but either way the math dictated Knox try to quadruple his money.

Even as he pushed in his chips and said, "The math says I call," Knox wondered if he should bother buying back in if he lost, or just go home and lick his wounds from the beating and stay the hell out of McKee in the future.

The little fellow drew his eyes tight and said, "Turn 'em up then," as he flipped his cards, showing 7/10 offsuit. He had two pair. His only hope of winning was to make a full boat on the final card, the river card. He could tie Knox's hand and chop the pot if another jack fell, but that was it. He only had four cards to win and two cards to tie. Statistically unlikely, but by no means uncommon. Knox had been fucked that way enough times to wince at the prospect.

Knox exhaled as he turned his jacks. The little fellow shrugged, looked at the dealer, and said, "Burn and turn, Rockhead. Maybe I'll catch me one." The man had been reckless, but showed no sign of regret. The dealer tossed a card into the muck in the middle. Then he turned a hapless 6 of diamonds onto the pilled green felt. "Well, shit," the little dandy said. "I made my straight." And he had, though lower than Knox's. He directed a single nod Knox's way. "Good call."

■ ■ ■

There's equity in sitting on a big stack won honest that can't be had by buying in high. Earned money is stronger money. Knox had run his initial two hundred to well over four hundred and that was worth something. Stack-size alone could win certain hands from certain players. Short stacks were liable to push in at any time, but most medium stacks didn't much want to tangle with a big stack if they could avoid it, unless of course they had a real solid hand to double on.

The big stack at the table had grown to a shade over five hundred. After that, there was Knox. The slick little guy had rallied back up to over three bills playing his same hell-bent style. He seemed to cow most everyone at the table, and more than just in cards. The paste sculpture behind him, who they called "Greek," behaved like a dog on a leash. The few instances when someone took a pot from the little guy, they wouldn't look at him. Like they were apologetic, but nothing was ever said out loud. The other players called him "Burl."

The table stayed juicy and loose. Knox's stack climbed mostly slow, and on the way up hit a couple snags. The lady whipped him with a full house after he had flopped trips, but she didn't have a real deep stack. He also traded chips with Burl here and again, but still, Knox climbed. He never got too deep if he didn't have a made hand, because Burl almost always showed down. Burl seemed fixated on getting his chips back from Knox specifically. That was the way of a lot of players. They held little grudges.

Once Knox had earned back his lost chips and then some, Burl scrutinized his near five- hundred-dollar stack. "I'd like to break into Fort Knox over there. That's what I'd like to do." Burl smiled then, but not friendly. "Boys, what do you all think of a man comes to a game the first time and makes hisself a bad guest?" Everyone else looked Knox's way and grunted softly.

Knox measured his words. In most other instances he would have told Burl what to fuck and where he could do it, but he knew better than to say it there. "I've caught some cards tonight, that's for sure."

"That you have." Two fresh cards went out and Burl took a look, measured out a preflop raise, and the subject dropped.

The game ground on until the small hours of the morning. A couple players busted and slunk on down the stairs. Knox yawned again and again, and the yawns grew larger and larger until other people at the table couldn't help but take notice.

The chinstrap kid said, "You might oughta hurry up, Burl. Fort Knox looks like it's fixing to close."

"That so?"

Knox tapped the screen on his phone, which was on the felt, and checked the clock. Then he looked at his stack. He'd made his way over six hundred and was the big stack by a third. "I probably ought to head to the house before too much longer."

"Hell, I ain't even broke in yet. Surely to god you ain't gonna leave with all my money and not give me no chance to get it back."

Knox pointed at Burl's chips, which were substantial. "You've had a fair night yourself, chief."

"Sure," he said, "but some chips is more special than others."

Knox picked up two of his own, flipped them between fingers one over the other. He looked up like he'd just thought of something. "Who is this we're listening to, anyway?"

Burl tilted his head a touch to one side. "You like that? That's Wayne Hancock. Still plays it like it was meant to be played."

"Is this an album?"

"This one playing's *Thunderstorms and Neon Signs*. It's a goodun."

"How many songs left?"

"Five or six."

"I'll stay till it's over. After that I got to go."

Burl checked some fresh hole cards. Then he tossed chips in underhand. "Come on in this water then. It's real nice."

■ ■ ■

Knox wasn't too eager to put his chips in harm's way. He tried the best he could to fold his way out the door, but didn't have much choice but to play when he caught ace/2 of diamonds in the big blind when nobody had raised and the small blind folded. The big blind was a forced minimum bet, so folding without a raise didn't make any sense. Burl and the lady in the denim shirt had called, so there were only three limping into the hand, a rarity at that table. When Knox tapped the felt, signaling his check, Burl said, "Fort Knox ain't closed just yet."

The flop came: king, ace, deuce—the king and deuce both spades. If Knox was beat at that point, both of the other two would have had to be slow-playing a big hand. The only way to find out was to throw in a little bet. There was fourteen in the pot, so he matched it. The woman said, "Well, I missed," and tossed her cards in disconcertedly.

Burl let his eyeballs run all over Knox while riffling his chips. "You make you a hand or you chasing that flush?"

Knox met his gaze. "One way to find out."

"Reckon." Burl flipped fourteen into the center as if he were sowing grass seed. Neither watched the turn card come off.

Their sights stayed on each other. The turn brought a queen of clubs. Burl glanced at it for no more than a wink. Then he scratched his nose, examined his fingers, and scratched it some more. "What do you think about that purty girl?"

There was plenty that could beat Knox's aces and deuces. All strong hands. Aces, kings, queens, ace/king, ace/queen. If Burl was sitting on two spades, he could still hit his flush on the river, too. Knox ran back the night trying to recall if Burl had slow-played any big hands. He couldn't remember one time.

Knox wanted to lead out with another bet and see if Burl would go away, but feared Burl might go up over-the-top. If he did, Knox would have to think about dumping the hand, which pained him. There were forty-two dollars in the pot, but since pot-sized bets seemed to beckon Burl to call, Knox dialed down to thirty, thinking that might spook him if he thought Knox was betting for value.

Burl ground his jaw like he was working a piece of gum, though he wasn't. He didn't say one word, didn't do anything, just looked at the chips in the middle and caressed that agate cross section he used to protect his cards. He said, "I call," then sat there a bit longer before extracting his chips and flipping them into the middle.

The river card was on the felt right on the heels of Burl's chips going in. Almost as if the card had silenced it, the country album timing Knox's play ended. Nobody stirred, nobody made a sound. For the first time, the drips from the kitchen faucet that had been pelting the dirty dishes in the sink all night were audible. The card was the ace of spades. A card worthy of such quiet. A card that made Motörhead play in Knox's mind, and made him study the other haggard faces at the table and wonder if any of them heard the same tune. It was a card that brought answers, but not all Knox needed. Not nearly.

He had a full house. Aces full of twos. Burl couldn't have two aces in the hole because Knox held one, so quad aces were out. Burl could have been playing for a flush and made it, but Knox had that beat. Knox also knew that the ace of spades hitting made the flush play less likely, as fewer players chased any but the ace high "nut flush," but with the hands Burl played, there was no telling. There were two hands Knox feared: ace/king and ace/queen. As wily as he already reckoned Burl to be, he could conceive of him doing that. If he had, Knox was beat by a bigger full house.

The simple fact was, Knox didn't know what Burl had. He'd bet into Burl twice already and figured out nothing. Knox decided to try another tack. He reached out slowly and tickled the felt with his middle finger, signaling a check, secretly

Knox ran back the night trying to recall if Burl had slow-played any big hands. He couldn't remember one time.

hoping Burl would do the same behind. They'd show it down and, win or lose, Knox would get out with a decent profit on the night.

Burl started talking. "You make your flush there, Fort Knox? Is that what you done?" Knox shrugged.

"You slow-play aces? You do that? You wouldn't do that to me would you, hippie-pizza-man? Just when we was getting to be friends." Knox shrugged again.

"Kings? Queens? You make you a big healthy hand?" Burl nodded. "I know you ain't got two queens cause that's what I got. I got queens full. You done let me lay around too long." He took a peek at his cards, whistled, and smiled. "Ain't they purty. You wanna see 'em?"

Burl slid his cards out and peeled at the corner like he was going to show, shook his head, and brought them back. He leaned back in his chair, took a cigarette from a pack of Marlboro Reds he had sitting on the table, flicked a matte-black Zippo from his front pocket that flamed just as quickly as he opened it, drew hard on the cowboy killer, and blew out the smoke swift and long. "I'm all in."

Knox pushed his lower lip into his upper, and his upper into his nose so his mustache hairs tickled his nostrils. "That's a bold move."

"No it ain't. It ain't bold at all when you got what I got."

Here's where Knox went into circuital psychology. In poker, strong is weak. Everybody knows that. Because everyone knows, there are people who act strong who are strong, thus giving reverse-reverse signals. But if Burl knew this, and he knew Knox knew, he could have been doing reverse-reverse-reverse psychology. So Knox was in limbo. He was pretty sure Burl didn't have the queens he said, but then again he might. Knox had seen it done. In that particular hand, Burl would be better off with only one queen and an ace. In a matchup of full houses, the higher top three cards determine the winner. Knox had aces full of twos: three aces and two twos. If Burl really did have two queens in the hole, he had queens full of aces, and it lost. That hand may have looked prettier, seemed bigger, but it was a loser.

To buy a little time, Knox asked a relevant question. "How much you got left in your stack?"

Without the slightest pause Burl said, "Four hundred thirty-five," puffing on his cigarette without touching it. Pasteurized milk–skinned Greek was peering in, trying to get a look at what all was out on the table, the whole time never uncrossing his bowling-pin forearms.

If Burl won the hand, Knox's big night was lost. He'd give back all he made and then some. It was supposed to be his last hand. He didn't have the best possible cards. He didn't have the nuts. He also didn't have a feel for whether Burl had him beat or not, but Burl gave off like he thought he did. The question that struck Knox was, if Burl wanted to take a chunk, why push him out of the hand? Burl had played the hand slow, and now at the end he was shoving it all in. Was that to extract the maximum, or to get what he could without showing down the hand? Knox wished for the answer, but didn't have it. Lacking the answer, and without too terribly much in the pot, the smart move was to fold and take home the hefty winnings he would have left. He needed that money. His parents needed it. Math didn't compel Knox to stay in the hand. He was lost in it, so he should've just gotten out. That was smart the thing to do.

The faucet continued to *drip drip drip*. Knox said, "I call." ■

MATRYOSHKA
(I SEE MY OLD AGE IN THE FACES OF THREE WOMEN LIVING IN CHERNOBYL'S EXCLUSION ZONE)

I love my native lands and I love my graves.
   —*Hanna Zavorotnya,* The Babushkas of Chernobyl

Babushka No. 1

When you unfurl your head scarf,
I half expect *dupa*[1]-length hair;
instead, you wear it thinly-cropped,
the grey cut close to the flesh. I
suppose it's easier this way,
to sever the reminders that youth
has passed, that our time has come.

At 31, I return to my hair the *kosa*[2]
my grandmother taught me to plait,
that symbol of maidenhood
I am too stubborn
to forsake.

Babushka No. 2

Your son died at 32, and you
buried him inside the Exclusion Zone.
You announce the memory
of your son's death with a brashness
I learned during my childhood afternoons
spent playing cards and sipping tea,
sucking caramels and drying clothes

with *Titka*³ Rita, who reminded me
not to whistle because *It
makes the angels cry.*

Four months shy of 32,
I have no sons, a choice
I made to spare them
—and me—
the questions, the strangeness,
the explanations as to why
their father can't understand.

Once, on Ivan Kupala,
I dreamed I bore a son
He emerged from me, his hair
cut in a *chupryna*⁴, his right ear
already pierced, a silver *tryzub*⁵
dangling from the lobe.
My son, he shook his fist
at the ground. When I
looked at his right hand,
I saw he carried his grandfather's *shashka*⁶.

---

1   Ukrainian word for "buttocks" or "ass."
2   Ukrainian word for "braid."
3   Ukrainian word for "aunt."
4   The traditional Cossack haircut.
5   The Ukrainian word for "trident."
6   A straight sword carried by most Ukrainian Cossacks.

Babushka No. 3

You dance in your garden, your flowered head scarf tied
around your face, your arms spread.
You greet the sun, point the soon-to-exist rows, announce
kartoplya[7], *kapusta*[8], *buryak*[9], *ohirok*[10].
You tell the sky *This is mine. This is Baba's* as you recount
how, upon returning three days
after the explosion, you put *Ukrayina's* soil into your
mouth and declared *Ya nikoly ne pokyne*[11].

I envy you because you held on your tongue what I
never could, though I know our alphabet, our enunciations
and pronunciations, though I can sign my name in two
languages—and often do—to remind myself home can be
5,100 miles from embering mountains that cannot
translate the schema my ancestors sculpted in my bones,
my eyes, the roses on my head scarf that I touch as I lean
against an oak tree, its branches pointing downward into
my hair, whispering *Dochka, ty nikoly ne poyidesh*[12].

NICOLE YURCABA

---

7   Ukrainian word for "potato."
8   Ukrainian word for "cabbage."
9   Ukrainian word for "beet."
10   Ukrainian word for "cucumber."
11   Ukrainian for "I will never leave."
12   Ukrainian for "Daughter, you will never leave."

CREATION MYTH

After Ken Burns's Country Music, *episode one*

What if the world wasn't spoken into existence
but sung, chanted, passed down?
Chicken one day, feathers the next.
It must have been obnoxious,
all that yodeling at the end of every sentence
while Experience coated the ground.
There was a time when radio
caused entire households
to dance right through the floor.
Maybe it really was all incanted or hammered out,
and then I came crawling, confused,
through a tobacco field in New York.
Spit 'er up, Jimmy! my hand said to the Sun,
Why should the devil
get all the good tunes?

CLAYTON SPENCER

THE FAITH OF WITHERED SEEDS

I try and exit
      quick the body
my lips

move like moths
      at the center
of the apple

from the center
      of the orchard
a blue diamond

reflects my startled grin
      how to plant silence
like an antique

pack of seeds
      found in the folds
of an encyclopedia

without instructions
      for care
in the Garden

I watch the moon
      lay itself across You
I watch white petals

wrap Your head
        I watch a man kiss You
the way I once kissed You

goodnight

CLAYTON SPENCER

DUNGANNON IN RELIEF

So all I have are snatches
of a dream I can't remember:
roads drawn as if by fingers
in the dust, hills with sun-stiff peaks.

Escape and tell the story
that you know, some ancestor
must have said, but no one did.
I'm still not sure if anyone

remembers it; that is to say:
I don't exactly know
if my mother's siblings sneaked
beneath the honeysuckle bushes

by the rails to feel the hum
of coal trucks in their ribs.
Whoever planted us
went underground, curetted light

from out the mountainside,
and had none left
to write their history by.
Still Mamaw traced the tracks

to work after my mother—
seventh child of I-
don't-know-how-many
came-and-went before—

was born into a Sunday,
Father's Day, and couldn't
hear him say, "Just look
at that baby smiling at me."

That's how the story goes,
what little of it I know.
Come winter, shocks
of snow like blown glass

banked the gullies. Help rose
like a poltergeist. All the world
went fickle, pony tired.
That is to say what's left,

what comes to mind, is this:
the bloodshot whites
of light-eyed men in dark
relief, their industry smeared

on their cheeks; the dreamy
sighs of dreamy girls
unsure why they can't chart
the map of stars they feel

they're made from.
When the boulder fell
(or the mine caved in,
or when William Howard

covered for a friend),
the money wasn't there
to say it in the papers.
Or, that is to say, Virginia

is for lovers, which we
were, but talk's not cheap.
Who wouldn't want
to find our stone-cut eyes

trawling the church aisle,
or sink into the cream-cool creek
and pull the leeches
off each other's supple feet?

However it goes, we're tilled earth
retching poppies; or, we're transplants,
perennials adapted to the heat.
We must believe in something—

call it tragic inevitability,
or early-onset discontent.
Maybe we've lost to history,
(maybe it's just me),

but still something goes on,
spangling the quiet dark.

CHEYENNE TAYLOR

STORM WATCH

I have just enough
of instinct left to know

these signs of rain:
an insect too routine

for memory flits
sideways; a squirrel

reports his body's
arc into the greasy breeze

between a low stone
wall and a shade tree.

The dish-pale sink of sky
sucks out a lottery

of robins worrying dirt
with pagan symmetry;

the drought-drunk grass
unfurls like local fame.

A thin electric tremble
coils the navel;

the bulk of us forget
each other's names.

CHEYENNE TAYLOR

MOVING HOME

Old men sing themselves
to sunstroke in idling

vans, their grown children
inside buying out

of season vegetables. We treat
our youth like succulents

on blistered windowsills,
the memory of sustenance

enough for us. We keep
flattening the dust, the way

a highway grinds the shade
to pulp, a longitude line

on a dry-erase globe.
Insects dither the coughing

of our sleep, our parched
throats spasming in heat.

At night, rapt in apnea,
we repel the dreams

where we steep in a neighbor's
tub water, retrace the peach

grey ring of a strange body's dross
so longingly with our toes.

CHEYENNE TAYLOR

MYSTERY
BEFORE MASTERY

LEATHA KENDRICK

I really don't know how poetry gets to be written. There's a mystery & a surprise, and after that a great deal of hard work. —Elizabeth Bishop[1]

What has always interested me about Bishop's statement is its declaration that a poem is "a surprise"—which I take to mean "an act of discovery." I don't believe that Bishop is talking about the kind of sudden intuition that often leads us to write a poem—that flash of understanding or brilliant (to us, at least) phrase that often sparks a poem. Bishop's poems probe and question—they lead me to unexpected places, word by word, observation by observation. They prove what Robert Frost said about surprise in poetry:

> *It is but a trick poem and no poem at all if the best of it was thought of first and saved for the last. It finds its own name as it goes and discovers the best waiting for it in some final phrase at once wise and sad. . .No surprise for the writer, no surprise for the reader.*[2]

Elizabeth Bishop's poems often discover mystery by listing. Take her poem "Filling Station," for example. The poem opens:

> *Oh, but it is dirty!*
> *—this little filling station,*
> *oil-soaked, oil-permeated*
> *to a disturbing, over-all*
> *black translucency.*
> *Be careful with that match!*[3]

Despite the "disturbing" "oil-soaked" aspect of the grubby filling station, Bishop does not flinch but continues to look, examining the filling station's cement porch with its "set of crushed and grease-impregnated wickerwork," which forces her to notice "on the wicker sofa/a dirty dog, quite comfy." Why all this close observation? What does she think she will see?

---

1   Elizabeth Bishop & Alice Quinn. "The Art of Losing." *New Yorker* (March 28, 1994).

2   Robert Frost, "The Figure a Poem Makes," *Collected Poems, Prose, and Plays* (New York: Library of America, 1995).

3   Elizabeth Bishop. "Filling Station," *The Complete Poems: 1927-1979* (New York: Farrar, Straus and Giroux, 1979), 127-128.

Ah, but the point for Bishop is to not avert our eyes, even from what she'd rather not look at too closely. With her the point is to simply look, and looking, to be brought to wonder.

In her essay on Elizabeth Bishop's "Filling Station," Molly Peacock speaks of the function of description—of listing objects, sense impressions or remembered events—in this way:

> *When you can't make sense of the world in any*
> *other way, merely to describe what you see before*
> *you leads to understanding. . .Description becomes*
> *knowledge. Details inform you of the shape of the*
> *world. Shape means perspective. If you are in a state of*
> *disorientation, you will gain a point of view. A point of*
> *view makes a sense of humor possible.*[4]

One thing that seduces me in Bishop's poems (like this one or "The Moose" or "At the Fishhouses") is her way of examining what might easily be overlooked and finding there layers of image and memory, humor and, finally, mystery. Bishop looks long enough to see not only the oily furniture and the dingy doily, but also the "big hirsute begonia" and the embroidered flowers ("marguirites") on the doily. Each a potential source of beauty, the doily marred by grime, the begonia by its heavy, hairy leaves. Bishop simply lists what she is noticing, until she sees both its beauty and its ugliness.

What she has noticed brings her to question what is behind the scene:

> *Why the taboret?*
> *Why, oh why the doily?*[5]

And here the poem has moved from its ironic, half-laughing opening vision of the filling station, oil-soaked and run by a father in a "monkey suit," assisted by "several quick and saucy/and greasy sons" to something unexpected. Simply by looking long enough to see what is there, Bishop has taken the poem to another level—both in tone and in content. She has written herself into surprise. And as she pursues her questioning, she realizes the care and the intention that keep the plant alive, that placed the doily there and arranged the oil cans "so that they softly say:/ESSO—SO—SO—SO/to high-strung automobiles." Attention itself is an act of love.

Frost also famously said that a poem should "begin in delight and end in wisdom," this poem begins in a kind of distaste and ends in transcendence: "Somebody loves us all." It achieves this motion from darkness into light because Bishop questions what she sees. Peacock notes that

> *part of the watching way of life is watching again. . .*
> *The poet models changing her mind, deepening her*
> *description. . .[making] revisions, modifications and*
> *corrections as the focus sharpens. . .correcting. . .the*
> *wrongness of immediate impressions.*[6]

For me as a writer, the function of making lists as a way to begin a poem is to invite attention to the particular, the concrete objects and textures of the scene or event. Looking—and looking again, we begin to question what we thought we saw.

Jack Gilbert's poem "Failing and Flying" finds its way to an unexpected conclusion in this way. Gilbert questions accepted wisdom as he examines the aftermath of a failed relationship.

4   Molly Peacock, "Joy: 'The Filling Station,' by Elizabeth Bishop," *How to Read a Poem and Start a Poetry Circle (New York: Riverhead Books, 1999), 164-178.*
5   Bishop, ibid.
6   Peacock, ibid.

The poem begins with a surprising line, "Everyone forgets that Icarus also flew." It continues

It's the same when love comes to an end,
or the marriage fails and people say
they knew it was a mistake, that everybody
said it would never work. That she was
old enough to know better. But anything
worth doing is worth doing badly.[7]

Gilbert invokes clichés ("people say . . ."), setting us up to see a reality beyond the expected. He inverts an aphorism to insist that even a failed marriage is "worth doing" and proves his point with a list of ordinary moments from the end of the relationship: "Every morning she was asleep in my bed . . .," he marvels. Gilbert somehow allows us to fall in love with the relationship that's over, simply by making us see what he saw: "Each evening I watched her coming back/. . ./the sea light behind her and the huge sky/on the other side of that"—as if the world coalesced around her silhouette.

Even the stars can (will) fail, he insists, watching how "love [was] fading out of her/the stars burning so extravagantly . . ./ anyone could tell you they would never last." By the end of the poem, he has convinced me that "Icarus was not failing as he fell,/but just coming to the end of his triumph."

In each of these poems, the poet enacts a reversal of the feeling created by the act of naming what is seen until the unseen flashes forth, embodied in what the poet describes. Each poem "finds its own name as it goes," to quote Frost again. Each poem "discovers the best waiting for it in some final phrase."

What can we learn from these poems? First, to quiet ourselves and look long enough to find the mystery behind what we think we know. Secondly, to use the power of lists. The third thing, and the key lesson, though, is to question the experience and revise our vision.

Go back to an unbeautiful moment or scene or to a failure. Begin by making a list that describes the unwanted circumstance, the thing you have avoided seeing. Be expansive: think Whitman! Be minute: think Dickinson!

Not knowing how to go forward—or what the moment might mean, look and look again. Question what you are seeing. Find the beauty and the unbeautiful. Ask why, as Bishop does, or why not, as in Gilbert's poem.

Draft a poem of twenty to twenty-five lines using images from your lists. Include at least one question in the poem and one unexpected place (Provence!) and maybe even an aphorism. Let the poem find its name as it goes. Be surprised. ■

---

7   Jack Gilbert, "Failing and Flying," *Refusing Heaven* (New York: Knopf, 2007), 18.

LEFT IN THE LURCH

I could go on forever
    in this labyrinth of wood pulp,
        plucking beeswax stalks off sconces,

pulling & prodding at appendages
    of statues that appear to flinch.
        A rustle of paper

trailing shadows
    in the corner of my eye.
        Nerves turn into extinguished wicks

with a fist-full of bronze braid as
    the heavy curtain draws open.
        Light from the picture window

falls across a section of ancient history.
    Warily through the corridor of light,
        I pry at a maroon spine

scrawled in faded gold lettering,
    revealing a false panel
        in the oak shelves, shifting perspectives.

        A spiral staircase plummets.
    I find myself lodged
in a cobwebbed enclave

        of catacombs lined
    with faded self-portraits,
silver emblems of dead names

embroidered on the tip of the tongue.
The librarian shushes from the other side,
and the hidden door slams behind me.

JAY BUTLER

A BOUQUET

Iris
The calico's eyes
bloom blue-yellow
in the window sill,
alchemical gold.

Sunflower
Towering over wired archways,
these guardians of hoop houses
offer their bodies for butter,
oil, lotion, birdfeed, or biodiesel.

Poppy
Armistice & remembrance,
women who caught whiffs
of independence in a San
Franciscan back alley way.

Morning Glory
Unopened spirals
oozing dewdrops,
showing up right on time
donning periwinkle flare.

Azalea
Fancying shade near, or under trees.
or enflamed in one of Sylvia's poems—
every spring, Gran plucked a few, propped
them in green jars at the dinner table.

Redbud
Under the Japanese Red Maple,
the redheaded tykes played in the yard.
Under & around the dogwood,
the redheaded tykes played with each other.

Mum
Nothing satisfies the urge
like pinching a seedpod
between baby index & thumb
in budding memories.

Chrysanthemum
Shot up from rootstock,
these fireworks explode
spreading red across the dusk
of moonlit blue grass.

Dahlia
Their diameter ranges from Spanish thimble
to Aztec dinner plate. Bright spirals
in a gaping mouth of pink teeth
like the gaseous jaws of stars.

JAY BUTLER

FAR
POST

JENNIFER LEE

My lip is swollen like a bee sting. On the inside it keeps rubbing against my braces, sore. All I can think about is the salty flavor of the cut in my mouth, and I've been late to every class, my mind wandering down the hall, sucking on this sore. Last year whenever I got banged up people would stop me and say, Oh my god! What happened? Now they know what to expect and no one says anything. Not even Bret, who is at his locker. He is looking at me in a funny way, like he has a question but is afraid to ask.

■ ■ ■

At practice Coach Mark has us doing lemon squeezers, ab crunches where we lift our hips and shoulders and twist side to side. I've done thirty; my sides burn and my nose is starting to run. My eyes tear up from trying so hard. I flop down on the mat while the other girls keep working on the sets. No pain, no gain, Coach Mark says, but I've lost faith in that equation.

Coach says, What's got into you, Margaret? He always calls me that. I hate my name, a little old lady name that reminds me of orange marmalade. Oscar, my dad, named me Margaret. He never called me Meg, not even when I got to middle school and started wearing eyeliner and asked him to. Coach saying my name makes the tears come again, and I get back to work on the lemon squeezers.

Last night I told Bret I missed Oscar, said it like a little baby, crying, and ever since I can't stop. Can't stop thinking about him, can't stop crying. It freaks me out. He's been gone two years; why am I crying now? I don't want to have a boyfriend I tell all my deepest stuff to, not this stuff anyway. I just want everything to be normal, like it used to be.

■ ■ ■

I started going out with Bret spring of last year. He was a junior so we got to go to prom together. I was excited about that, but it wasn't the big deal everyone talks about. I had the ugliest dress on; I kept looking at the other girls, wondering why I couldn't have picked something pretty. Under those ballroom lights my dress looked like crap: a whole lot of puce-colored satin, tight in the wrong places, loose in others. I probably should have let my mom go shopping with me. She'd have known how to pick out a decent dress, but I was still mad at her for making me go to therapy. I've been seeing Sally on Wednesdays at five o'clock since May and it's a waste of my time. All she wants to talk about is my dad. She says it's normal to feel conflicted. I'd rather tell her about having mad sex with Bret, or make up something stupid like that.

■ ■ ■

Coach teases me about my lip, tells me to quit pouting. I'm off my game, and he's trying to figure out why. It isn't the pain; I don't mind that. This swollen lip is no different from the raspberries I get when I dive, the way the yellow bruises look when they come out days later. The worst was in eighth grade when some girl tore my nose with her spikes. Lifted that little flap right up off my nostril and I bled all over everything. My mom wanted me to quit playing, she said I had a death wish. Oscar had been dead a couple of months and maybe I was a little crazy, diving after balls I shouldn't have. But making plays in goal was the only thing that made me feel good, and no way was I going to quit.

My nose looked gross, all swollen and red with dried bits of blood it hurt too much to pick off. The stitches were like little black bug legs stuck to my face and I took my mom's nail scissors and cut them down as short as I could.

My mom hadn't been at the game. She wasn't even worried when I came home an hour late. She was sitting at the kitchen table drinking a glass of wine and talking on the phone when I walked in. I could tell she'd been crying so I knew she was talking about Oscar. Her own therapy—Pinot Grigio and a phone call. I told her the coach had tried to call her five times. I stared at her phone, trying to make her feel guilty, but she didn't get it. She held my chin, started crying again, and tried to tell whether the cut was going to leave a scar.

I thought it healed up pretty good over the next ten days; unless you pushed on my nose to look into that pink crease, you couldn't even tell I'd been cut. The doctor cleared me to play again when he took the stitches out, but my mom was thinking about plastic surgery. If we decide to fix it, she said, pretending she hadn't heard the doctor say I was good to go, can you straighten out this bump? She was pointing to the middle of my nose, a broad, bumpy part people say is from my dad. The doctor looked at her like she was crazy, closed his folder on me and said No.

■ ■ ■

I got good instincts. That's what Coach Mark says, and I know it's true. You got to in goal. You got to know when to come out, that's the most important thing. On a breakaway play, a lot of players will just kick the ball right to you, but if the girl has any skill at all she's going to put the ball in a corner

I got good instincts. That's what Coach Mark says, and I know it's true.

before you can even wave your hand at it. Coach says it's my good instincts that I know when to come out, but there's science to it, too. The second she touches that ball, you break. It's all about timing. A fast girl with instincts of her own isn't going to give you the chance to touch that ball. She will get to it again before you, and she will shoot. Your whole chance of stopping the shot lies in breaking down her angles. If you get your body horizontal and you're just a few yards away when she kicks, she's going to have to kick it right into you. And that's the science of the angles. It's just like a pool table, really.

These are the kinds of things I try to tell Sally, the things that make sense to me. She nods her head and smiles and lets me go on. Then she asks some question about Bret and I know she doesn't understand.

Sally wanted to hear all about prom, so I told her. I told it just like it was—disappointing and stupid. Bret didn't chip in anything for the hotel suite where we ended up after the dance was over. It was crowded and Bret loosened his tuxedo and did beer bongs until he was ready to puke. A bunch of girls sat on the bed doing shots. I stood around until they told me I could sit with them. They gave me a shot glass and a wedge of lemon. I felt ridiculous, dressed up and partying on a hotel bed with a bunch of girls I didn't know.

I drank two shots and then Bret came over and took my hand, and we went and sat in a chair together, started making out. It was weird making out with everyone around, but other people were doing it. The tequila and the beer flavors tasted weird mixed up together in our mouths, and I was thinking more about that than kissing. A little later the guys who had paid for the suite started kicking everybody out. Their girlfriends watched them and waited, and I was glad we were leaving.

We pulled out onto Route One, which was almost deserted at two a.m. We were near the intersection of Randolph Road where we were supposed to turn when Bret pulled into the parking lot of a Red Lobster. He parked in the dark, far back in the corner. He reached across the seat and started kissing me, wet and sloppy. He started feeling around the neckline of my dress, trying to get his hand inside.

Bret stopped making out with me as fast as he'd started. He opened his door and threw up on the pavement. When he was done he sat still for a minute. Sorry, he said. He was too embarrassed to even look at me. He rolled his seat back a little ways and fell asleep. I rolled my seat back too, until I was looking at nothing but the worn ceiling of Bret's mom's Honda Accord, listening to the traffic and the ticking of the engine as it cooled.

Time was up when I got to the end and Sally looked relieved our session was over.

■ ■ ■

Breakaways are easy to play compared to the rest. When it's just you, you don't have to factor in what your defenders are doing, and there's no one obstructing your vision. When to come out on a corner is a tougher play. Most goalies just stand there and watch it happen, let the defense do all the work. But a good corner kick is a goalie's play, at least if you're tall or can jump at all. And it's a great place to use your fists, because you don't want to flub a catch right in front of the net. Most goalies are too scared to push through all those people, five or six attackers crashing your goal, and you're going to have to jump right on some girl to get the ball. But your fullbacks are on the posts when you go for it. Defending a corner kick is a team effort, and you got to count on your teammates to do their jobs.

Soccer is my therapy, I told Sally in the beginning of August. Tryouts had just finished and I had made varsity. Why do you think soccer is your therapy? Sally asked. I hate it when she turns everything I say into a question.

■ ■ ■

My mom tries her hardest, I know she does. If I had a subscription to *Seventeen* nagazine I think we would get along better. But we're like on different astral planes or something.

My mother's perfume—you can smell it before she enters a room. And she has big, high maintenance hair, frosted with streaks of blond. I didn't get that gene, the super feminine glamour gene. I'm the sort of girl who'd wear dirty sweat pants from the bottom of the laundry basket rather than a dress to school. I don't think my mom is disappointed in me, she just doesn't know what to do. I can't blame her. She counted on Oscar being around to raise me.

We were a normal, happy family; everyone would have said so. Then Oscar OD'ed, took pills and drank and didn't wake up. My mom says it was an accident and I want to believe her but sometimes I wonder. I wonder who Oscar really was. I remember him the way kids remember their parents; he's just a picture in my mind, an action figure in my life. I try to imagine how he saw me, but I can barely remember who I was two years ago; it was the beginning of eighth grade, and I was still figuring out how to wear a bra. When my dad died of an overdose everyone knew. Everyone looked at me in that special, awful way reserved for tragedies. No one knew what to say so no one said anything. I wish I'd been really little, like four or five, because then I wouldn't have understood how weird everyone was acting. But then I probably wouldn't remember Oscar at all.

■ ■ ■

The girls on my team like Coach Mark because he's good at what he does, but they make fun of him behind his back. They call him Madman because he looks like John Madden, the football announcer. Coach Mark is big and fat with thick blond hair, fleshy lips and fat fingers. You can fault him for not being able to do all the stuff he yells at us to do, but that doesn't really matter in a coach. A coach doesn't have to be able to do a damn thing. A coach has to be there every minute, see every play, know what every girl needs to do. That sounds obvious but it's not. I know because from the goal I see all kinds of things that need doing—like drop passing, for god's sake—but how do you get people to do that? Coach Mark yells his head off during the game hard enough to pop blood vessels in his eyes, and then afterward he's totally mellow, like he knows we'll never figure out any of the stuff he's saying until at least midseason anyway.

■ ■ ■

Sally's job is to listen to me talk, so I talk about soccer because that's what I know. But as soon as I pause she asks a question about Bret, or my dad or mom, or even Coach Mark and I get so mad. The last time I saw her was the day before the game, so I was keyed up and going on about how to stop big plays. She asked me if Bret was coming to my game and I leaned back and crossed my arms and said, Why does everything have to be about sex? She tried to do that therapist thing and flip the question back at me. Do you think everything is about sex? Sally asked. No, I said. I kept my arms folded and didn't say anything else for the rest of the session.

Even though I was thirteen when he died, my memories of Oscar are starting to fade. All I've really got are some photo albums and three shaky home videos of me blowing out birthday candles at different ages. I watch them sometimes to catch a glimpse of Oscar: he'll be standing behind me while everyone sings happy birthday, or the camera will pan past him as he's drinking a beer with the neighbor.

He named me Margaret after his mother. My name is a weak reminder of a man I barely knew, worse than a candle on a cake. Then last year in English class we read a poem that goes: "Margaret, are you grieving, over golden grove unleaving," and it sent a chill down my spine, like maybe Oscar had said those lines long ago when they couldn't have meant anything between us except my name. I was crazy about that poem, even wrote a paper on it. It was the only time I ever got an A in English class.

I thought about telling Sally this but decided not to. It's a special piece of me, that poem, and I don't want anyone handling it the wrong way.

■ ■ ■

Yesterday's game was our season opener. The first game of the season matters more than anyone realizes. It isn't the score, whether you win or lose, but the players on your team are either going to impress you or depress you in that first game. I was worried about it. If I screwed up my team would think I sucked and start covering my position. And then I wouldn't trust myself, which is the worst thing for a goalie.

I was jumping up and down in little stiff-legged jumps, gritting my teeth. Nobody noticed because each of us was busy doing our own version of being stressed out. Coach Mark saw me though. He came over and put his hand on my shoulder, kept me from doing my little jumps. Margaret, relax, he said. Imagine all the shots you're going to stop. Really imagine them, one after another. Take your time to really feel it. Imagine your perfect game. I started breathing deep and I stopped hopping around. I got my mind under control. For some reason I always need to be reminded of the shots I'm going to block; I can't seem to master my nerves on my own.

I stood on the line waiting for the start of play, breathing deeply through my nose and imagined myself tapping a wicked corner kick out over the top of the goalpost.

McLean is good. They have some of the fastest players in the county, girls who've played club soccer since they were eight. I had to bust my ass the whole game because we couldn't seem to keep the ball at their end for more than a few seconds at a time. We had nothing going on the ground, our passing game was nonexistent, and they picked off every ball in the air. I'd trap it and punt it straight to my girl, crossing the field and sending it just past the midline. All she had to do was step into it. But every time some McLean girl was faster. She'd put a head on it and once again the ball was in their possession.

■ ■ ■

After the game I went with Bret to the bonfire party. It's a big tradition, and I wanted to go to the bonfire party worse than I had wanted to go to prom. Parents and teachers have known about the party for years, I don't know why it isn't more secret, with kids lighting fires and drinking, but no one has ever put a stop to it. My mom banged around the house, slamming things down hard when I told her I was going with

I'm not young, I said. I'm in high school, or haven't you noticed.

Bret. She kept saying how I was too young, that the bonfire party was for older kids. I'm not too young, I said. I'm in high school, or haven't you noticed. I could see by how her lips went thin that she was tired of arguing with me. If your father were here, she said, you can bet he wouldn't let you go to that damn party. Well, I said, my own lips getting thin, he's not here, is he.

There were logs rolled up close to the fire for people to sit on. There wasn't much to do but listen to music and drink flat beer. The only upperclassmen I knew besides Bret were a couple of girls from my team. After our McLean game there wasn't much we had to say to each other. Bret left to throw a football in the dark with a bunch of guys. I thought about following him, but sitting on the log in front of the fire made me feel sleepy.

■ ■ ■

I saved way more shots than I could possibly have imagined, but the one I remember is the one that went in. A tall girl, number nine, had been pounding me the whole game. She had the speed and the footwork to bring the ball down the field all on her own. Over and over again she would fake out the defenders, bringing it in closer until the only people between her and the net were me and Carrie Ford, the sweeper. Carrie's good, as good as this McLean girl, and she forced a lot of weak shots. But ten minutes left in the game she's tired, and number nine gets past her and takes the shot that counts. She's not a girl to miss an opportunity, and this one flies straight for the far post, low and hard. I came out and threw myself across the line of shot, but the ball got past me. The score was one to zero. We deserved to lose the game by a lot more, but we'd all been hoping to pull off a tie. After the game Coach Mark put his hand on my shoulder. You can't stop all of them, Margaret. You know that, right? You did good out there.

I knew it. But I hated the way I felt, like maybe I could have stopped it. This is the psychology of the missed shot, guessing how things might have turned out had they gone differently. It hurts so much. I figure that's why so few people ever want to go in goal. It has nothing to do with getting hit. Personally, I've loved playing goal from the minute I started playing soccer way back in kindergarten. Oscar used to take me down to the park Saturday mornings and we'd practice together, him rolling the ball fast on the ground, teaching me to get my body behind it. There aren't any photographs of us doing that, so I know my memory is real, I didn't just make it up from a picture.

When I think about that missed shot, every missed shot, really, I can't help but think what it would be like if Oscar was still here. When he died I had just become a teenager, really getting into the stage where I hated my parents. Being with them in public was embarrassing and all I wanted to do was stare at the computer and pretend I was someone else. I don't even know if I talked to my dad the day he died. I wish I could go back in time, wake up and jump on his bed like I was five years old, watch him laugh and cover his face with a pillow like he used to do when I was little.

■ ■ ■

I was thinking about Oscar and the shot that got past me when Bret came back. He was sweaty from playing football and he smelled nice, the way a clean boy smells when he sweats. He took my hand and we walked off toward the trees, away from the light of the fire.

In the dark he leaned down to kiss me, his hands under my breasts. Ow, I said, that hurts. What hurts? He asked. Everything, I said. My lip was pretty swollen, and Bret had been careful about that, but I hurt everywhere else too. Until Bret touched me, I hadn't realized.

What do you want to do? he asked. I could tell he was disappointed. I thought of letting him touch me even though it hurt, but the thought of doing that made me want to cry. All of a sudden I wasn't sure if I was able to talk, or what I would say if I could.

What did I want to do? I wanted to do what I hadn't done. I wanted to stop the shot, talk to my dad. I wanted to rewind everything, back before the game started, when I could still imagine victory. I wanted to see Oscar again, trap the ball when he drilled it hard and low toward the net, just the two of us on a green field, a crisp morning in autumn that lasted forever. Instead, every part of me was a bruise. I used to think pain was a cup I could pour everything into. It kept me going, for a while. Now my cup was broken, and all the tears I had poured into the pain rained down. I couldn't stop it. ■

BOOK REVIEWS

Margaret Renkl. *Late Migrations: A Natural History of Love and Loss.* Minneapolis, Minn.: Milkweed Editions, 2019. 248 pages. Hardcover. $24.00.

Reviewed by Greta McDonough

Late Migrations arrived on a busy afternoon, and I took a moment to flip through it, so inviting was the artwork, the dust cover, the heft of the nice paper upon which it was printed. I read the first essay and then the next. I was rooted to the spot, unable to put it down; I read deep into the afternoon and until the light failed.

Late Migrations, Renkl's book debut, is a work firmly rooted in memory and stories, contemplations and meditations on the author's beginnings in Alabama. It is a book threaded through with observations of the natural world, the one found in red clay roads, creekbeds and suburban backyards. The collection carries the subtitle *A Natural History of Love and Loss*, giving the reader a glimpse into a childhood in a specific place, keen observations of the habits of bees, wolves, dogs, and especially birds, bundled together in a voice that is anchored in the here and how, the wise everyday, of someone who is paying attention.

The essays are short, some just a page, others shorter that. This bijou is presented with poetic brevity and from time to time she shares the stories passed down to her from her grandmother. These are written in italics, reminding us that the voice, the actual voice is stilled—but the memory lives in these pages.

Renkl, of course, has stories of her own to tell, and she does with clarity, honesty, and heart, reminding herself of our attachment to and alienation from the natural world. She writes movingly of homey things like chicken and dumplings, Christmas ham and the "beds that birthed babies." She takes us on a creek walk with her younger brother, their feet hardened by a barefoot summer outdoors, showing us that creek and remembering how the subtle smell of decay wasn't even worthy of curiosity then.

We visit her backyard in Nashville, where she now lives, and she shows us the bird feeders by every window and a white pine too close to the house—the one she forbids her husband to take down when he contemplates it because it reminds her of home. We know their yard is unruly compared to the neighbors.' But it sounds lovely, there in the middle of a large city, and we wonder—if we ourselves drove slowly and paid attention—if we might also catch a glimpse of wildness in the midst of urban life.

One theme of *Late Migrations* is the struggle of holding together both the wild and the tame, abundance and decay, the sorrow of loss and the joys of living. It is no easy feat, and

Renkl reminds us of this over and over. "Again and again I have to teach myself the splendor of decay," she writes in the essay "Farewell." This, alone, is a superb sentence. But in Renkl's deft hands it becomes something more, and so begins a meditation on the order of things, an essay truthful and hopeful, and complete in the span of a mere ninety-seven words.

That is the thing about these essays: there are over a hundred here and each one stands alone, complete and lovely. They remind us of ourselves, our parents in their prime and our parents in their leaving. We hear the howl of an old, beloved dog, that most faithful of family members, and we begin to grieve him before he leaves us, loving more fiercely what he once was and what he has become. We think about the bees and the clover Renkl plants and the incredulity of her neighbor who spends good money to get rid of it in her own yard. We linger every twenty pages or so over the beautiful artwork that graces the pages. (The muted, jewel-like drawings are the creations of her brother, Billy Renkl, a collage artist.)

While each essay stands on its own, taken together they create a moving and honest memoir, one with the central themes of nature, both wild and orderly, and the loss and grief of letting go, something she foreshadows in the epigraph she has chosen. It contains two quotes, the first from Arthur Miller's Death of a Salesman: "Well, dear, life is a casting off. It's always that way." And then, from George Barker, "Therefore all poems are elegies."

If this gives the impression that this book is morose or depressing, nothing could be more wrong. It is a mature book, to be sure, one that could only be written from the vantage point of a writer of a certain age. In an interview with novelist Silas House, Renkl was asked about her purpose for writing the book, what she most wants readers to get from it. She says she started writing about her own feelings of loss when her mother died suddenly of a cerebral hemorrhage. We live with much loneliness and homesickness and loss, she says, but in a time of quick fixes and glib reassurances, those things people say to us to minimize our pain or try to convince us that it will—or should—pass quickly. None of this is helpful, according to Renkl.

She says we have arrived at point in time when suffering is seen as an anomaly and joy the norm, thereby fueling the impetus to move quickly through and away from sadness and grief. This is a mistake, Renkl believes. The goal is to hold the two together, in acceptance and hope.

She began, then, to write about what she was feeling, thinking, in the hope that others might find it helpful, as writing it down was helpful to her. She speaks humbly of this, in the voice of a kind and trustworthy friend who would never presume but who stays close and quietly hands you tissues, or tea, or any of a hundred small things you might need in that moment.

This is *Late Migrations*. A hundred small essays, a thousand observations, a meditation on the wider world of nature as a way to inform the smaller spaces of the human heart. Renkl is a compassionate and wise companion, pointing out where to look, just there, under those branches, beneath that pine, under the mossy rocks of a stream. Her voice soft, kind, knowing. Her writing is smart and moving, yet clear-eyed and devoid of sentimentality, a tricky balance to strike when grappling with personal material.

I read *Late Migrations* in one sitting. I read it fast so I might turn to it again to savor it slowly. I have the lay of the land, having read it from start to finish, and now I dip in and out of it when I need to be reminded of something she has said, or when I need help listening to my own stories of loss and hope. It's that kind of book. A wonderful read, beautifully crafted, and more, much, much more.

Michael McFee. *Appointed Rounds: Essays*. Macon, Ga.: Mercer University Press, 2018. 224 pages. Softcover. $20.00.

Reviewed by Emily Masters

"Writers wield such flimsy materials for immortality—the ink that fades, the paper that yellows or crumbles or burns, the books that waste away on dusty shelves, unread," Michael McFee writes in "Immortality," the final essay that closes on the most touching theme perforating his collection *Appointed Rounds*. McFee's desire to be remembered and fear of being forgotten with time is one to which everyone can relate. The theme feels essential to humanity yet can also somehow feel isolating which McFee perfectly captures. Throughout the collection, there's a tension at play between acknowledging the likelihood—and perhaps even grace—of eventual forgetting and the heart's plea for recognition, for someone left behind who will sing praises of a life well-executed and well-written.

McFee maps onto the pages of *Appointed Rounds* his fears of being forgotten and desire for remembrance just as much as he maps the routes of his writing life and the North Carolina streets he has called home for a lifetime. He practices remembering the places and people he has called home the same way in which he hopes to someday be remembered, with complexity and, often, with reverence. The essays are broken into bits and pieces, sections mirroring the frequent stops of the United States Postal Service from which he takes inspiration for his title.

While McFee addresses a variety of topics in the collection, the essays are first and foremost about his writing life and how to find beauty in the surrounding world. He visits the late Reverend Billy Graham's library in "Just As I Am Not," and feels out of place when he notices the lack of books in the "library," making him feel even more alienated as "a lapsed Baptist, lapsed choirboy, and lapsed architecture student who became a writer." In "Anthologizing," he sees his reading life as a constant picking and choosing, saving old favorites and adding "concentrated verbal worlds that have spun into view for the first time or returned for another appreciative viewing." He finds beauty in the structure of books as physical objects throughout the first of seven sections in the collection.

McFee is, first and foremost, a poet, which is made obvious by the short sections and lyrical qualities of his essays. The essays in the collection read more like poetry than essays at times, and occasionally readers may feel bogged down on a word-by-word level, sucked into detail instead of feeling immersed in the narrative as a whole. The pages will turn quickly due to the flow of the words and the white spaces between sections playing easy on the eyes.

As a poet and essayist, McFee finds art in the everyday: in daily walks to the mailbox "pausing by the sprawling rosemary bush, which I pinch for postal good luck" in "The Mail," in old friends in "For Doris" whose "fierce dark eyes pierced, sparkled, didn't miss a thing," and, most notably, in the way he wrestles words "patiently, painstakingly, deliberately" in "Proofs." The wrestling of words will resonate with writers struggling to tame their work into something tight, something beautiful. His writing is a lesson on how to view one's surroundings in a writerly way.

McFee's focus on his writing life can at times feel like instructions in craft. He details the process of making a book, of receiving one's newest publication in print, of creating a writing routine, and even feeling guilt as a writer who can work from home while his wife spends the day away at her job. Because of this, these essays will feel more relatable, more in sync with readers who also write than with those selecting a book for pure pleasure.

At his best in the collection, McFee whorls words onto the pages which will sweep readers up with their loveliness and considerate placement. However, there are moments in the collection which begin to feel a bit self-congratulatory or self-promoting. Nowhere is that more evident than in "My New Yorker." McFee celebrates his poem "Snow Goat" published in the New Yorker, a cause for celebration and pride, to be sure. Unfortunately, dwelling on the past achievement and republishing the poem in the collection feels like too strong a push for remembrance.

As someone who shares McFee's affinity for letter writing and receiving, my favorite essay of the collection is "The Mail," a meditation on the personal qualities inherent in the deeply involved process of writing, sending, delivering, opening, and reading pieces of mail. A letter is a laying of soul on paper, a gift, an offering to commune with those about whom we care. He presents, here, his essays as offerings to the reader, lying in wait to be opened, read, remembered.

Marc Harshman. *Woman in Red Anorak.* **Amherst, Mass. and Seattle, Wa.: Lynx House Press/University of Washington Press, 2018. 70 pages. Sofcover. $17.95.**

Reviewed by Ali Hintz

In *Woman in Red Anorak*, Marc Harshman's third full-length poetry collection, the poems span over disparate times and places, from a post-apocalyptic America to the Allied invasion of France to the afterlife in an old woman's backyard. While these jumps can be disconcerting, they serve to illuminate the universality of human experience. He explores the value of words in a world full of scarcity, loneliness, and war.

The title poem caps off the first part of the book which deals with wars both in the flesh and mind. A man, home from war and suffering from PTSD, dissociates for hours in a forest until his mother calls out for him. In his vision, there is "a woman in a red anorak standing with him,/ standing in the middle of a sea just before a storm." The identity of the woman remains unexplained.

In the first poem, the post-apocalyptic "Parts," the speaker describes relationships

> *between those with broken hearts*
> *and the handsome toymakers*
> *who could still remember how to fix them.*
> *And would have fixed them,*
> *if only they could've found the parts.*

The characters populating this collection try to fix what cannot be mended, such as the mother of fallen World War II soldiers in "Restless" who "once could mend anything" but now searches for "another pattern,/that one we all reach for/ wishing to bring back the dead from dying." Hope is scarce here, even when aided by love.

The mother, this time a grandmother, knits in the background of prose poem "Keep Calm." Set in the near future, her son wonders how to tell his family war is coming. "How does he tell them about the change that has come, arrived here this very moment? What words will carry the weight of this heavy earth, the million depths, the little, strangled cries? What words carry on?" Harshman continues to explore the meaning of words in times of crisis throughout the book.

One of those words gets its own poem: "Trust." The speaker starts simply by telling the reader, "You know this word." The poem goes on to enumerate the ways trust can be used and abused in some of the most beautiful, sharp language in the book. The ending lines, "Still, it is patient,/ and waits for you,/ when all the other words are gone," lend a little hope to a book full of despair.

The third section features a breakup between long-term partners. In "Such Little Light," a woman is alone in the forest thinking about what to do with her partner's fury. Words, and the lack of them, play an integral role to her solution. She hears him call out to her, and "Feels good, very good, to hear him, and hear herself not answering." Her silence speaks more than her words could. She is tender with her fury, although she decides to let it, and him, go. "The echoes of a thousand words of comfort she lifts in her hands and gently blows them into the cotton mist lifting into the hollow. It's a lot to give after all these years. It's enough now with which to leave." By giving up the words of comfort shrouding his fury, she frees herself. As the summer night falls around her, she looks to the fireflies for guidance. The fireflies are "in love with nothing more particular than warmth and darkness. To think such little light could lead a path." "Such Little Light" is true to its name, providing a little light to the reader, who at this late point in the book needs it.

The woman needs and uses words to let her partner know about her decision to leave in "She Didn't Have Much to Say." She texts him, her words indirect yet still a "swift dismissal/ of the old ways and the distances between." The man responds with characteristic anger:

> *There might have been some other words,*
>   *but there were none would burn any brighter*
>   *than these turning blue*
>   *under his fists.*

Words, then, are a vehicle for his fury and her freedom.

In the final poem, "The Company of Heaven," the reader returns to the grandmother's home. In the most bizarre moment of the book, a jet lands in her backyard, and she welcomes its polite occupants into her home. The stewardess calls her name and the grandmother realizes she is in the afterlife. She is nonplussed and says to herself there is "no use trying to explain it." Words cannot explain the miraculous, the divine. She muses, "a hundred years from now, who knows how the story would be told." By not trying to shape the narrative, she decides to give herself up to that which is greater than her. "She's glad for the company, though, and if they plan to travel on, she means to join them."

So, what words do carry on? Harshman wrote a book about the words that are unspeakable, the words that carry our lives. Words that fear, that love, that trust. Harshman's words search through difficult times and places to find that one word underlying human life: hope. ■

RECKONING

You keep your failures close, intimate
as unwashed sheets—that colleague's
novel left untouched in its box,
a dead friend's *corpus* of poems
that will not see print,

an ex-husband who can't
be shaken loose,
a lover who comes close
but not closer.

Here is your photo gallery:
mountain landscapes emptied of people,
still life of moss and rocks,
a crayfish surprised outside its burrow,
desperately waving its single claw.

VALERIE NIEMAN

LIMITED CREATURES

He is an outlier as well for all I know, another seizing an opportunity
likely to be all-too-rare in weeks, as the ice lays claim to open water,
swooping down from his grey and bony precipice to grasp a remnant
(something left behind by his careless neighbors) and a shivering nod
toward warmer and longer days, the muted hum of slower waters.

There is cold comfort (the best anyone can hope for) in the notion
survival tests the limits of all God's creatures, even those with razors
set at the end of their feet. This and the belief we share something,
if only the fact we are both here after all the others have departed,
testing our limits against some perfect storm of circumstance.

My hands burrow in my pockets as I lean into the wind, admire the arc
by which he returns to his jagged outpost to consume a moveable feast.
It is difficult for me to conceive of him as endangered, vulnerable
to the poison compromising the veneer protecting his offspring.
The trouble with me is a lack of exposure, too little time spent basking

D.E. KERN

(or better yet grasping) the brilliance and exhilaration lent by light.
I pay entirely too much attention to the cold, musing on the way
it consumes us from the ground up and exposes suspect foundations.
These days are too short. This sun is too kind. And I'll shriek my song.

CONTRIBUTORS

Wes Browne is the founder and host of Pages & Pints Reading Series at Apollo Pizza in Richmond, Kentucky. He lives with his wife and two sons in Madison County, where he practices law, co-owns and helps manage local restaurants and a music venue, and coaches sports. His debut novel, *Hillbilly Hustle*, is published in March.

Jay Butler holds a B.A. in History & English with a concentration in Creative Writing from Appalachian State University. He is a member of the Southern Appalachian Writers' Cooperative and his work has appeared in *Pine Mountain Sand & Gravel*.

Annette Saunooke Clapsaddle, an enrolled member of the Eastern Band of Cherokee Indians, resides in Qualla, North Carolina. Her debut novel, *Even As We Breathe*, will be released in Fall 2020. Her first novel manuscript, *Going to Water*, received The Morning Star Award for Creative Writing from the Native American Literature Symposium and was a finalist for the PEN/Bellwether Prize for Socially Engaged Fiction.

Annie Frazier lives in North Carolina and received an MFA in fiction from Spalding University in 2017, where she served as Social Media Coordinator for the program and as a student editor for *The Louisville Review*. Her fiction and poetry has appeared in *Paper Darts, Hypertrophic Literary, Longleaf Review, Cabinet of Heed, Philosophical Idiot, CHEAP POP, Still: The Journal, Crack the Spine, apt magazine*, and *North Carolina Literary Review*.

Richard Hague is the author or editor of twenty collections of poetry and prose, most recently *Earnest Occupations: Teaching, Writing, Gardening, & Other Local Work*. He has received the Weatherford Prize in Poetry, and Poetry Book of the Year from the Appalachian Writers Association. Forthcoming soon is a collection co-edited with Sherry Cook Stanforth, titled *Riparian: Poetry, Short Prose, and Photographs Inspired by the Ohio River*.

Ali Hintz is a queer poet and farmer from Appalachian Pennsylvania. Her work has appeared or is forthcoming in *Pine Mountain Sand & Gravel; Miracle Monocle Anthology: Queer, Rural, American;* and in other publications. She is currently an MFA candidate at the University of Arkansas where she has received Walton Cole and Distinguished MFA fellowships.

Silas House is the nationally bestselling author of six novels, most recently *Southernmost*, as well as three plays and one book of creative nonfiction. He is a frequent contributor to the *New York Times* and serves as the NEH Chair of Appalachian Studies at Berea College and on the fiction faculty at Spalding University's MFA in creative writing.

Leatha Kendrick is the author of four books of poetry, including *Almanac of the Invisible*. Her essays, poems and fiction has appeared widely in journals and anthologies, including *The Baltimore Review, The Southern Women's Review, Appalachian Heritage*, and in other publications. She leads workshops at the Carnegie Center for Literacy and Learning in Lexington, Kentucky, where she is part of their Author Academy faculty.

D.E. Kern is a writer from Bethlehem, Pennsylvania. His work has appeared in *Glint Literary Journal, Reed Magazine, CRATE, Hypothetical: A Review of Everything Imaginable, Autumn Sky Poetry Daily, Wilderness House Literary Review, Nude Bruce Review, Negative Capability, Limestone,* and *Mission at Tenth*. He teaches English at Arizona Western College.

Jennifer Lee is a graduate of the MA writing program at Johns Hopkins University and an editor at the *Baltimore Review*. Her stories have appeared or are forthcoming in *Phoebe, Bellevue Literary Review, Monkeybicycle, Jabberwock,* and elsewhere. Her work has won the Maryland Writers' Short Fiction Award and has been nominated for a Pushcart.

Emily Masters is a graduate of Berea College and serves as book reviews editor for *Appalachian Heritage*. She is from Monteagle, Tennessee, where she lives on a farm with her family. Her work has been published in *Still: The Journal* and *The Pikeville Review*.

Greta McDonough is the author of *Her Troublesome Boys: The Lucy Furman Story*. She writes a popular weekly column, "From this Place to That," for the *Owensboro Messenger-Inquirer*, and her writing has been featured in *Kentucky Living, Still: The Journal,* and *Appalachian Heritage*. Her photography has been exhibited at the Loyal Jones Appalachian Center at Berea College and featured in *Kudzu* and *Still: The Journal*.

Valerie Nieman's fourth novel, *To the Bones*, is a genre-bending satire of the coal industry and its effects on Appalachia. She is the author of three poetry collections and her writing has appeared widely in journals and in numerous anthologies. A graduate of West Virginia University and Queens University of Charlotte and a former journalist, Nieman teaches creative writing at North Carolina A&T State University.

Tina Parker's new poetry collection will be published in late fall 2020. She is the author of the poetry chapbook *Another Offering* and the full-length poetry collection *Mother May I*. Her work has received support from the Kentucky Foundation for Women and has appeared in *Still: The Journal, Pen+Brush, Rattle, Literary Mama,* and *PMS: poemmemoirstory*.

Clayton Spencer is a worker, a poet, and a Kentucky-Appalachian. He holds a B.A. in English from the University of Kentucky and currently lives in Columbus, Ohio.

Cheyenne Taylor is an MFA candidate at the University of Florida. Raised in Alabama by a Virginian mother and a British father, she received her BA and MA in English from the University of Alabama at Birmingham. Her poems have appeared in *Barrow Street, The Cincinnati Review, storySouth,* and *Quarterly West*, among other publications.

Terrance Wedin's work has appeared in *Esquire, Fourth Genre, Ninth Letter, Washington Square Review, Hobart, New South, New World Writing,* and other publications.

Nicole Yurcaba, a Ukrainian-American writer, teaches in Bridgewater College's English department, where she also serves as the Assistant Director for the Bridgewater International Poetry Festival. Her poems and essays have appeared in *The Atlanta Review, The Lindenwood Review, Chariton Review, Still: The Journal*, and many other publications. Yurcaba lives, gardens, and fishes in West Virginia with her fiancé on their mountain homestead.